# Enlightene‹

"Get ready to move your dog interactions to a new level of consciousness! Jesse Sternberg sheds light on the most prominent dog behaviors and issues that many canine guardians are faced with each and every day. This wonderful book is filled with valuable tools and resources that will undoubtedly help you to cultivate a loving, respectful, and peaceful relationship with your beloved companion. *Enlightened Dog Training* is the perfect antidote for dog lovers seeking a more conscious and enlightened way to train their canine companions."

**– Tammy Billups**, certified interface therapist, teacher, and author of *Soul Healing with Our Animal Companions* and *Animal Soul Contracts*

"Jesse Sternberg's *Enlightened Dog Training* is a revelation not only in how we humans communicate with our pets but also how we interact with the entire animal kingdom surrounding us. Revealing the secret language used by animals across the planet, Sternberg provides dog caretakers with unprecedented wisdom, training, and know-how to become confident peaceful alphas of their pack and masters of communication with the natural world."

**– Jonathan Talat Phillips**, author of *The Electric Jesus* and cofounder of the Evolver Social Movement

# ENLIGHTENED DOG TRAINING

## Become the Peaceful Alpha
## Your Dog Needs and Respects

# JESSE STERNBERG

FINDHORN PRESS

Findhorn Press
One Park Street
Rochester, Vermont 05767
www.findhornpress.com

Text stock is SFI certified

Findhorn Press is a division of Inner Traditions International

---

**Disclaimer**

The information in this book is given in good faith and intended for information only. Neither author nor publisher can be held liable by any person for any loss or damage whatsoever which may arise from the use of this book or any of the information therein.

---

Cataloging-in-Publication data for this title is available from the Library of Congress

ISBN 978-1-64411-370-7 (print)
ISBN 978-1-64411-371-4 (ebook)

Printed and bound in the United States by Lake Book Manufacturing, Inc. The text stock is SFI certified. The Sustainable Forestry Initiative® program promotes sustainable forest management.

10 9 8 7 6 5 4 3 2 1

Edited by Nicky Leach
Text design and layout by Richard Crookes
This book was typeset in Avenir Book

To send correspondence to the author of this book, mail a first-class letter to the author c/o Inner Traditions • Bear & Company, One Park Street, Rochester, VT 05767, USA, and we will forward the communication, or contact the author directly at **www.peacefulalpha.com**.

With love to my pack,
Noah and Jordyn

# Contents

# Prologue

It was 6:30 a.m. on a Friday morning, and I was already in the zone. The crisp air of a Canadian autumn left a sting on my cheeks from the walk into work with my furry business partner, the inspiration behind everything: my beloved four-year-old sheepdog Maydel. At that time of day, I felt perfectly comfortable allowing my sleepy companion to roam the sidewalk behind me unleashed.

She followed me loyally, ignoring the garbage wrappers, squirrels, and joggers that used to tempt her with far too much excitement for my liking. I trusted her, and she trusted me. I made a point of not watching her like a hawk. Had I done that, my body language would have told her that she was doing something wrong and resonated the feeling of fear. This would have accomplished nothing but diluting my Peaceful Alpha power.

Though I kept my back turned on Maydel for the majority of the walk, I wasn't being mindless. I could hear her collar jingling as she moved faster or slower, depending on what her nose was catching along the way. My shaggy guru had earned that kind of freedom with me. I knew that I could call her to come to me at any moment. I also knew that she was very likely to make a deposit somewhere that would need to be picked up. So even though it appeared as if I was aloof (a genuine characteristic of an Alpha), my attention was fully locked into the conditions of the present moment.

As usual, I meditated while we walked. My posture was tall and relaxed and my feet kissed the earth with each step. My movements flowed with a rhythmic grace and my heart-mind was reverberating in a yummy coherence of benevolence. This is how animals move when they're feeling tranquil, so naturally this is how a Peaceful

Alpha ought to move as well. How else can we demonstrate to our dogs that we speak the Secret Language of Dogs? Little did I know it at the time, but my work with canines was transforming me. I was becoming a very sophisticated animal myself, and in doing so, I was becoming supernatural.

By 6:45 a.m., like clockwork, we'd make our way down the narrow alley that led to the back entrance of my shop. I loved entering the store at this hour. It was always so quiet, clean, and zenlike. I unlocked the door, turned on the lights, and went across the street to grab a quick coffee. Technically, we didn't open until 7 a.m., but oftentimes I'd return to find two or three dogs that had checked themselves in. These clients were regulars and didn't need to see me. That was Maydel's early morning job. Furthermore, I had installed discrete one-way dog doors and pre-trained these clients for such occasions.

It was now 7:15 a.m., and a swell of 11 familiar dogs had already arrived and settled in. I had had my coffee, the incense had been lit, and soft classical music was serenading in the background. I was organized, energized, and viscerally present, sitting in my meditation chair in the back corner of my doggie daycare. Nine of the dogs were clustered around my feet. They were sitting or lying in the shape of a semicircle. It felt like our consciousnesses had merged, amplifying the vibe of tranquil alertness in me.

Not only had I not said a word to them since they had arrived, I hadn't touched them nor allowed the angle of my upper torso to line up directly in their path. Instead, the majority of my attention was channeled toward the bells, which were hanging on the front door. One of the responsibilities of a Peaceful Alpha is to demonstrate protection of the territory. Judging by the relaxed energy of my pack, I clearly had this base covered.

Though the lights were on in the shop, new clients driving by would have been initially confused because, as usual, there was no one up front in the reception area. I didn't like to bring staff in until

9 a.m. Those first two hours were sacred for me. It was when I set the tone for the dogs for the entire day.

Over the next few hours, the phone would ring up to a dozen times and another 10 to 15 dogs would arrive. I'd interact with the clients when they dropped their pets off, make bookings, and listen to grooming instructions. While I was doing all of this, I was careful to silently play the angles with the pack, demonstrate mastery over the territory, and attune myself to the dogs' Calming Signals. You see, dogs only exist in the present moment—I could never turn off my communication with them.

My tone of voice, posture, and emotional energy stayed in constant communication with the canines, even though it seemed as though I was oblivious of them. If (and when) they acted up, my use of timing, touch, sound, and the Forbidden Angle gave me considerable power of influence to rebalance them emotionally and take them back into a calm state.

Should these not work, I'd simply put some fresh kibble into a single bowl in the middle of the room, but I wouldn't let any of them touch it—at least not at first. When you control the resources, you also control the energy. As dogs would calm down and focus on the powerful scent they were attracted to, I would reward only the ones who went through the full Sequence of Surrender and lay down with their chins on the floor. These actions communicated to the pack exactly how I expected them all to behave.

This was my morning routine, six days a week, for nearly a decade. As my business matured, I was able to build a great team and evolve my line of work. I'm not quite sure how it happened, but word got out and I was sought after as a master dog trainer. With no formal education in the field, I never really considered myself to be what people thought I was. Instead, I liked to view myself as someone who teaches people how to communicate with their dog.

My approach was to introduce my clients into the realm of animal consciousness, resource-guarding theory, territory management, hypnotic training exercises, and of course, the Secret Language of Dogs. In my heart, I knew I wasn't teaching people how to train their dogs; I was spreading light, leveraging the Law of Attraction, introducing cutting-edge meditation techniques, and attempting to lead like a gentle soul.

It is my opinion that no dog ever thinks that they are the one who is misbehaving. That's something we project onto them. I also believe that dogs are very empathetic, highly conscious, and incredibly attuned to their owner's emotional fields. Our dogs are literally our reflections; they absorb our unconscious "baggage," if you will. If we're anxious, they're anxious. If we're stressed, they're afraid something is wrong. If we're loud, looking at our phones, or tuned out, they lose faith in our ability to keep them feeling safe (yet they still love us, this never ends).

I've come to see that any problematic behavior our dogs exhibit—whether it be lunging, jumping, whining, or barking—is simply the canine's attempt to act out these unpleasant emotions from their body so that they can rebalance their own energy. A calm dog is always a good dog. This is true even if the canine doesn't know any commands nor has had any training whatsoever.

This book is about learning how to behave so that you earn your dog's respect and communicate with them at their own level. My goal is to provide you with refreshing and simple tactics you can use to transform your dog into a stoic, well-tempered, naturally obedi-ent companion. You will find case studies of normal people and the everyday problems they are having with their dogs. The stories are layered with practical wisdom and take the reader on a journey of developing their own Peaceful Alpha power while solving their pet's behavioral issues with ease and a little common sense. Each chapter includes an illustration, some enlightened training tips, and a meditation to solidify the lessons.

I genuinely hope this book inspires you, opens your heart-mind, and leads to a deeper bond with your dog.

# 1

# Becoming a Peaceful Alpha

In my early twenties, I was reading a lot of Deepak Chopra, and his wisdom from the *Seven Spiritual Laws of Yoga* gave me the faith and the courage to start my own business. In his book, he invited readers to follow their hearts, be of service, do what they love, and trust that the Universe will take care of the rest.

I knew that I loved dogs. Their energy always uplifted my spirit. Back then, I suffered from anxiety and depression, and the joy of being around dogs calmed my heart. Diving head first into my dream of working with them, I decided to trust Deepak (and the Universe). I opened a dog daycare and grooming business in Toronto, Canada, and soon everything in my life began to change.

I started my journey into the world of canines by researching the traditional sources of authority on dogs: puppy parents at the park, breeders, veterinarians, reality shows, and groomers. Though they were incredibly experienced with canine wisdom, I felt that there was something more. I consumed every training book I could get my hands on. I studied what the monks of Newskete did with German shepherds; how to "Be the Pack Leader," according to *The Dog Whisperer*, with Cesar Millan, a celebrity dog trainer with a show on National Geographic; and how Jesus would raise a dog, if he had one, by the author of the best-seller *The Original Dog Whisperer*, Paul Owens. I spent countless hours immersing myself in videos online, scrutinizing all the various modalities I could find, including positive reinforcement, rally competitions, obedience, search and rescue, special needs therapy and *schutzhund* (a competitive form of guard-dog protection).

By experimenting with many different modalities in my dog daycare business, I quickly began to see that no single methodology worked reliably or consistently. Different dogs within the same breed would often respond unpredictably to the same training styles. In fact, the truest thing I noticed was that as more dogs were introduced into the equation, the less any of the training techniques seemed to work. There was something about the modern idea of "dog training" that just wasn't delivering the results I was expecting.

Observing groups of dogs together at the leash-free dog park, or in my daycare, it was easy enough to see that canines are able to communicate silently and respectfully with one another. I'd often wonder if every dog owner wanted to know how to have a real conversation with their dog. I couldn't have been the only one.

## Discovering the Secret Language of Dogs

In the spring of my second year in business, there was a perfect storm of events that forever changed the course of my life. It had been torrentially raining for several days, and most of our clients were unable to walk their dogs in the mornings. The bad weather brought in tons of new daycare dogs, and fortunately for business (but unfortunately for my anxiety), we got a lot busier. A manageable pack of 15 dogs had suddenly swelled to 36 maniacal furry beasts.

The dogs were literally bouncing off the walls. There seemed to be no end to their lunging, jumping, barking, scratching, squeaking, attacking each other, and defecating everywhere! My stress levels were reaching an all-time high. None of the training modalities I had been studying were successful in calming or controlling a pack of that size. In fact, every time we tried to connect with the dogs using traditional methods, it inflamed the energy of the room, making the pack even more hyper and unpredictable. My biggest fear, that someone's dog would get injured in my care (or die), cycled uncontrollably through my thoughts.

Sitting in my office, taking a moment of reprieve from the noisy pack, I heard a few sounds that put me over the edge. Bang. Squeal. Silence. The sequence of these sounds scared me sober. It unexpectedly brought me into a state of pure presence. It felt like the transcendental experience I had read about in my Buddhist studies, but to date had only caught minor glimpses of in my meditation practice. When I entered the main play room to investigate what I had just heard, I saw everything with a fresh mind. I realized that Izzy, our best client (a young but incredibly hyper chocolate lab), was chasing other dogs at lightning speed. Like a hockey player who uses the boards to stop, she had intentionally slammed herself into the wall to change her momentum. Luckily she was okay. The bad news? She blew a hole in the drywall and completely disrupted the business next door.

Somewhere between laughing and crying, my experience of space-time seemed to bend into a new reality. The voice in my head quieted, sounds became clear, and I could suddenly feel the dog's emotions as if they were my own. As clear as day, I observed the dogs in the pack communicating with each other in their own way. Henry, the old golden retriever, was yawning at the puppies—not because he was tired but to calm them down and reassure them. In dog language, the yawn can be used (among other things) as a social signal to encourage relaxation. Marge, the shih tzu, looked away from the other dogs as she peed. Not because she was shy, but because this angle tells the other dogs to give her some space and peace.

The realm of feelings is where true animal communication takes place. I realized that dogs make quirky little gestures on purpose

**Figure 1: Calming Signals**

Dogs use a variety of facial expressions, body gestures, and angles to communicate at the emotional level. These signals are designed to eliminate unnecessary confrontations and keep the peace.

Shaking = Energy Changing

Looking Away = Being Peaceful

Cautiously Trusting You

- "Me Calm Down"
- "You Calm Down"
- "Environment Calm Down"

Lip Lick:
You Can Trust Me

Bow: Inviting Play

Turning Back:
Ignoring, Avoiding

In general, your dog communicates one of the following messages:

- I want to calm down.
- You need to calm down.
- Something in our environment needs to calm down.

because it generates emotions. By using specific angles, postures, timing, and sounds, dogs have actually developed their own vocabulary. As humans, we have never really had to tap into this, but I assure you, the potential is there for us to harness it.

Learning to communicate with dogs using this Secret Language of Dogs was actually much simpler than it sounds. Take a look at Figure 1 on the previous page to get a sense of what some of their vocabulary looks like. The best part about it is that it meant I now had a way to communicate to every dog that came into my establishment. Rather than spending all my time training dogs, I could simply talk to them in their own language. That old saying "You can't teach an old dog new tricks" suddenly lost all merit. My use of the Secret Language of Dogs generated results for me that were hundreds of times better than the conventional conditioning methods I had been studying.

## Transformational Effects

As I began experimenting with my ideas about this Secret Language of Dogs, I noticed all animals in nature communicated in this fashion in some way or another. Wolves, bears, and coyotes lick their lips to express Calming Signals. Cows, moose, even birds avoid direct eye contact, unless being intentionally confrontational. Squirrels are masters of the angles, and you can always spot an alpha of any species by their casual use of the posture of protection. The lessons I was learning from this secret language didn't just apply to dogs, they actually worked on humans as well.

As for my clients, they started to comment on how clean the daycare was becoming and how calm their dogs were when they went home. Customers sensed something special was happening. I was connecting to a new pack everyday and oftentimes transforming over 30 "bad" dogs at a time. These dogs would come in crazy and go home as zenned-out, obedient dogs. The most rewarding part about it was that these dogs genuinely loved me, and they also respected me. By communicating with them on their own wavelength, I was able to lead them, make them feel safe, and earn their respect. Naturally, when I commanded them, they listened in ways that made their owners curious. The same clients started asking me to help them with private training, and the effects they experienced were just like mine.

At the time I did not think that I was teaching my clients anything radical—simply learning how to tune into the realm of feelings is often the hardest part. With a little effort and some guidance, they were quickly identifying that most of their dog's bad behaviors originated when their dog feels too excited or too scared. The brilliance of the Secret Language of Dogs is its clarity. It is like learning how to speak in your dog's native tongue. As my private clients mastered the secret language, they found that their dogs started to treat them differently. They started to respect their owner's presence and desired to listen to their authority.

As my clients gained experience, they were able to connect with their dogs in new ways and do all kinds of remarkable things they had only ever dreamed about. They could open the front door, and not only would their dog not attempt to escape it would calmly fan away from the door and lie down. They learned how to walk their dogs with a loose leash, and some of them with even no leash. When they called their dog, it listened. When they told the dog not to touch their tuna sandwich, it didn't even dare look at it. Inevitably, a big shift started to take place. My clients began trusting their dogs more (and worrying less), and they also became calmer, wiser, and more compassionate in the process. It's like their dog was teaching them to become a better person.

The key to all of this was the meditative approach they were taking to connect with their dogs. The more peaceful and attuned they were to their own emotional energy, the more receptive they became to the communication signals coming back to them from their dog. As they did this, my clients would not only become the Peaceful Alpha their dog both needed and respected, they also became a grounding, supporting, loving leader to their family and friends. For many, their health improved, their careers blossomed, and their personal and professional relationships flourished.

In essence, all of our dogs' behaviors are really just a reflection in some way of our own unconscious emotional baggage. As you take focused action in improving your dog's behavior, you can't help but grow into the Peaceful Alpha that both you and your dog have always dreamed of you becoming.

# Training Tips
## Becoming a Peaceful Alpha

1. There exists a Secret Language of Dogs that we can tap into to connect with our dog, change their behavior, and achieve incredible results with ease.

2. Most of your dog's behavioral issues are emotionally based: they are either too excited or too scared; therefore, the simple solution is to communicate with them and help balance their emotions.

3. It's easier for a human to learn the Secret Language of Dogs than it is for dogs to learn English (or any other language). Mastery of their secret language will make you more peaceful, calmer, and happier. It will also transform you into a better person.

4. Three critical components of this language include:
   - learning how to relate to resources and territory;
   - learning how to speak in the actions your dog might make;
   - deepening your level of presence and attunement to your dog.

# Meditation

## Your Dog Is Your Guru

Sit comfortably, or rest on your back. Allow your breath to flow naturally. Just be still, and channel your attention into your body as it breathes away on its own. Be a watcher. When your dog lies in stillness on its side, resting in a patch of light coming through the window, it is being a watcher. Watch the sensations you are feeling come and go like waves in the ocean. Feel them now, know that they will soon flow away. Know that there's another layer of consciousness you will soon be accessing.

Resist any urge to dissect your emotions and try to figure them out. Your dog lives in the languageless realm of feeling sensations, and in a little time, you will join them there. Allow the talking mind to exhaust its efforts while you observe it in nonjudgment. Cultivate the discipline to stay with sensations as you forge a new kind of power born from nonreactivity. Come back to your breath. Come back to the feeling sensation of your lungs expanding and contracting. Focus your attention and feel your breath.

A guru is a very special teacher for a meditation practitioner. Their teachings arrive when you're ready to receive them. This often happens as you experience life together. Your dog is a master in conscious awareness, an expert in the art of present-moment living, and of experiencing joy, peace, and ease. Maybe the very reason your dog is here is so that they can bestow these virtues upon you. Your dog's presence and energy have the wisdom to elevate your emotional intelligence and bring you internal peace. Ponder this sacred relationship while you remain in meditation. Stay here for as long as you like.

# 2

# The Secret Language of Dogs

The key to understanding the Secret Language of Dogs is realizing that every action an animal makes has an intention behind it. Through her research on what she called Calming Signals, Norwegian dog trainer Turid Rugaas demonstrated that dogs lick their lips, yawn, raise a front paw, and even walk in semicircles on purpose. If you are wondering why they do all these things, and more, it is because they understand that each action generates a subtle emotional vibration in themselves and others. Once we become aware of this simple code, the depth of our empathy spontaneously starts evolving, because we love our dogs so much we never want to cause them any distress.

## Actions Create Emotions

When we give our dogs verbal commands, what they are primarily paying attention to is the emotion within our voice (its tone), our posture (is it confrontational or calming?), and our relative position within the environment (what is our status in, and our awareness of, the territory, and how we are making use of the angles?). They perceive all of this information at the vibrational level and they assess, overall, the level of goodness and truth in the authority of our command. In this sense, because dogs think primarily using feelings, you could say that their brains are in their hearts.

Figure 2 shows how this plays out in your dog's mind.

**Figure 2: Actions Create Emotions**

Let's explore what's happening in this diagram from both the human perspective and that of the dog.

Here, we have a human who has just commanded their dog to "sit." Oblivious to his body language, the owner is making some serious mistakes that are scaring his dog unnecessarily. He is staring at his dog, which generates fear; he is pointing at his dog's face, which intensifies the fear caused by the Forbidden Angle; and his spine is curved inward, which suggests frustration or anger. As we will discuss later, it's perfectly okay to engage in the Forbidden Angle to express a command, but lingering in this position unnecessarily creates anxiety in the dog.

Although the dog is sitting, it is not calm and relaxed. Not only is the dog trying to revert to its natural peaceful state (by yawning) but it is also using this social cue as an attempt to communicate to its master to chill out. Remember, when we give our dogs verbal commands, what they are primarily paying attention to is

- the emotion within our voice (its tone),
- our posture (is it confrontational or calming?),
- and our relative position within the environment (what is our status in, and our awareness of, the territory, and how we are making use of the angles?).

Animals do not really have labels for their feelings, but they do know that their experience right now is pleasant, unpleasant, or tranquil. This is the simple part that kids and dogs just get. When things feel pleasant, your dog tends to want to do them more. When they are unpleasant, then it tends to want to stop doing them. When things feel neutral (or tranquil), then life is awesome, and it is just as it is supposed to be for your dog. They appreciate the safety of this emotion and behave with a natural, joyous curiosity that Mother Nature intended for all of her creations. In these moments born of tranquility, your dog is incapable of being anything but a good dog (no training required).

The trouble with too much pleasantness or unpleasantness, though, is that there is an attachment that happens to the former and an aversion that accompanies the latter. Attachments and aversions take our dogs out of the tranquil state, and hence, trigger an emotionally charged response that leads to behavioral outbursts. Many dog trainers encourage owners to be "very excited" when they are giving commands to their dog, yet this is rather foolish because it only revs up the dog's emotional engine. The wise understand that an overexcited dog cannot also be a calm and obedient dog (in the same moment). Emotions must be acted out of the body, and this is the source of all kinds of undesirable behaviors (lunging, jumping, barking, and so on).

The vibration of tranquility is where all of nature desires to be, including humans. There is a security and peacefulness found in experiencing this vibration for long durations because it leads to blissful serenity and inner harmony. Another practical reason why we would want to become familiar with this tranquil feeling is because this is where your Peaceful Alpha power comes from. When we consciously send a signal that generates either love or fear (the feeling of pleasant or unpleasant), from a place of placidness, the contrast of the emotion from your dog's perspective becomes heightened; thus, the directive you are giving your dog will become clear. Please familiarize yourself with Figure 3 to get a sense of the basic emotions a Peaceful Alpha uses (on purpose) to be the master their dog both needs and respects.

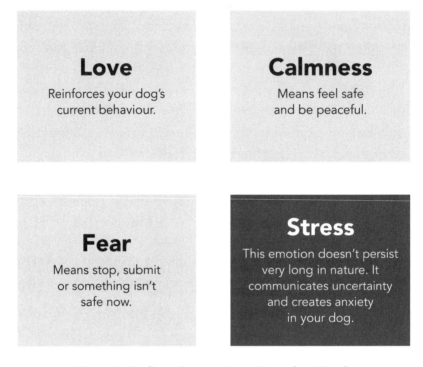

**Figure 3: Feelings Communicate More than Words**

Love, Tranquility, and Fear are the major feelings a Peaceful Alpha uses to communicate with their dog. Practice tuning into how you feel when you're around your dog. Do your actions line up with your feelings? If not, you're confusing your dog, and this leads to anxiety, frustration, and neuroses.

Let us take a closer look at how dogs use these principles on one another so that we can get an idea of the subtleness of this language and how it plays out, even when we are not intentionally using it. When we observe an older dog around a puppy, most of the time it is just calmly doing nothing while it lets the puppy explore, or do whatever it wants. Calmly doing nothing is actually a conscious action for a dog. The emotion it broadcasts to the puppy neither reinforces the puppy to do it more, nor scares it to make it stop; thus, the puppy receives the emotion of neutral presence and realizes that its behavior must be okay with the older dog. Communication can only take place in the present moment. Actions, even nonactions, create emotions.

Consider how, when we are on the phone and not paying attention to our dogs, they take our emotion of tranquility to mean they are allowed to keep chewing the baseboard or keep peeing in the bedroom. The key lesson here is that we need to show up and "be in the moment" in order to communicate with our dog. We make our first step toward becoming a Peaceful Alpha through the intention of being present.

# Calming Signals

Dogs communicate with their posture by making a myriad of gestures known as Calming Signals. Though there are many different Calming Signals, their meaning always falls into one of these three proverbial buckets: (1) Me calm down, (2) You calm down, or (3) Something in the environment needs to calm down.

### Your Dog's Most Essential Calming Signals

- lip licking
- yawning
- blinking
- raising the front paw
- lowering the head
- lowering the body

Consider the following three examples to get a sense of how canines communicate using Calming Signals.

1) **Me Calm Down:** An owner is tidying up the countertop and accidentally jingles their car keys. The pleasure of this familiar sound triggers excitement in their dog, which was sleeping on the floor just moments ago and now thinks it might be time for a joyride. The dog realizes that there is no car ride happening, so they yawn, not because they are sleepy, but because this action tells them to calm back down. The yawn actually triggers the biology of their nervous system to engage in the automatic process of relaxing.

2) **You Calm Down:** At the park, a small dog approaches a tennis ball they see lying inches away from a bigger dog. As the small dog gets closer to the toy, the big dog suddenly becomes aware of them. Stealing a toy is grounds for conflict, so the little dog communicates their peaceful intentions by raising their front paw. The little dog thus says to the big dog, "Don't worry, I am not going to steal it. I just want to check it out." The big dog sees this from afar and decides to stay tranquil by blinking at the small dog, saying, "Thanks for not disturbing me." The efficiency of nature's communication trumps every verbal language invented by humans.

3) **Environment Calm Down:** A dog senses a train going by on the railroad a half-mile away. The vibration of the ground wakes and alerts them and they lick their lips a bunch of times, communicating to those that are watching that something in the environment is disruptive.

If you're looking for a tangible way for you to see what your dog is trying to communicate, simply observe its Calming Signals. Your dog makes hundreds of these every day. With just a little practice, you will gain tremendous insight into your dog's emotional world. Interestingly, not every dog will use the same signals, and a particular dog will likely only have a few Calming Signals they consistently use. Regardless, we know that every signal can only fall into one of three buckets, so the more present we are, the more adept we will inevitably become at identifying these signals and intuiting whether the alert is: me calm down, you calm down, or situational. This is a really important first step. Just taking this action is enough to start earning some major loyalty points from your dog. You can cash them in later for better listening, calmer behavior, and more attentiveness to you. This is the way of the Peaceful Alpha.

## Power Angles

The next time you get the impulse to snuggle with your dog, try this. Look at them lovingly, attempt to hold their gaze, and observe what they do. My guess is that they will immediately begin showering you with calming signals you were formerly oblivious to, such as blinking their eyes, yawning, or licking their lips.

They are sending you these messages as a way of telling you to calm down. They think that you're angry with them, even when your intention is a loving one. If they choose to snuggle you back, they will likely angle their head down and away from yours, a conscious action that communicates the same thing as offering you their bum for a scratch.

The message here is simple: Your dog wants to be with you. They feel your love, but the emotion you're feeling (love) is not lining up with the unconscious feelings you're sending from your confrontational actions, which are signals for fear. This is why our dogs don't look at us when we're looking at them. Your loving action is making your dog afraid.

Why is this important? In the long run, sending a mixed message that combines love and fear is the recipe for creating all kinds of neuroses and anxiety. It is actually the culprit for future behavioral issues.

While we are often oblivious to this, your dog is not. This emotional miscommunication confuses your dog, and will cause them to lose respect for you, even though they will never stop loving you. Animals view humans as animals, and our postures serve as conscious actions that communicate with them. When they first get to know us, this is one of the things they're assessing. It is our biggest opportunity for conscious growth. The clarity of our communication when we get it right ensures that our dog will evolve into a stoic, calm, attentive, responsive dog.

# The Forbidden Angle

Making direct eye contact with another animal is taboo in nature because it makes them feel uncomfortable or threatened. This phenomenon is not just something animals experience; it is very real for people as well—our parents just trained it out of us.

When I was a kid, I hated looking at grownups and strangers. I found it intimidating. I do not think I'm alone in this. Direct eye contact generates the vibration of fear because it is rooted in ancient animalistic conflict-seeking intentions. This is why we naturally avert our eyes from that creepy person getting on the bus, and why it can be so difficult to reach out and shake hands with strangers.

Using the right intensity of eye contact, in the right moment, for the right reason, is precisely how we leverage our Peaceful Alpha power. Sometimes, we tend to avoid fear because we think it is bad; actually, it is completely natural for a dog to feel fear when another dog is telling them "no." It is also natural for us to feel this emotion, yet we have been conditioned to think that it is bad, so we avoid experiencing it as often as possible.

When communicating with your dog, a healthy dose of fear contains the exact amount of intensity required to motivate a behavior, no more and no less. Used unconsciously, however, or with too much intensity, it just scares your dog and results in them trusting you less. Do not worry. Tuning in to your dog's Calming Signals will motivate big changes in your awareness and physical behavior. Once you begin to see that you are accidentally scaring your dog, you would not want to continue doing so, right? This is but one of the reasons why your dog is your guru.

No wonder Calming Signals involve blinking, looking away, and lowering the head. These are conscious communication responses that intentionally break the fear generated from the Forbidden Angle. All animals are familiar with this code. We earn our dog's respect when we start embodying this principle.

## The Angle of Protection

The opposite of the Forbidden Angle is the Angle of Protection. Rather than creating fear, this angle generates feelings of safety and tranquility, which are actually just different expressions of love. When your dog feels safe, their body becomes calm. When their body is calm, they are not going to act out their feelings. It follows, therefore, that a calm dog is a perfect dog.

Leveraging the Angle of Protection simply means ensuring that we are always aware of, and closer to, the object of fear or excitement than our dog is. Our body becomes the energetic blocker: keeping our dog behind us while making eye contact with the oncoming object gives our dog an extra feeling of protection. Doing this consistently gives us incredible power because it says "I've got your back" or "No excitement right now" in a very relatable way.

Using the Angle of Protection not only demonstrates to your dog that you are on the same team but also suggests that you are the captain. We will explore these principles in greater depth throughout the coming chapters of this book, but in the meantime, take a look at Figure 4 for a little preview.

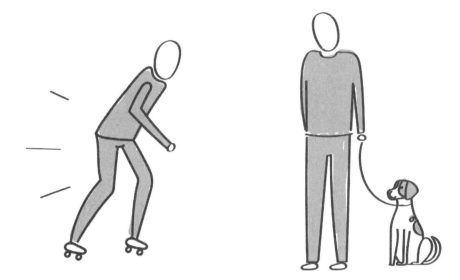

**Figure 4: Angle of Protection**

A Peaceful Alpha uses their keen sense of sight, which is superior to their dog's, to identify any Straight Line Encounters before their dog can. Remember, these perceived threats often trigger fear or excitement in your dog, and that is what makes them misbehave.

To keep your dog calm, simply place your body in between your dog and the object approaching. Your body becomes the energetic blocker. Another tip is to turn your back to your dog. This position not only assumes more of a leadership role but also communicates that you trust your dog and have their sense of safety in mind.

# Living and Learning These Principles

The next time you observe dogs interacting with one another, just look at the great lengths they go to ensure that the vibes of fear and its derivatives—anxiety, stress, and worry—never enter their environmental airwaves. The very nature of their Calming Signals ("Me calm down," "You calm down," or "Environment calm down") reinforces a tremendous layer of compassion for one another. Their communal desire for peace and tranquility is always leveraged through conscious actions, creating harmonizing emotions that have a net-calming effect. How beautiful is it that this secret language, from an animal's perspective, is based on compassion for one another's feelings. Imagine life on Earth if humans were as connected to one another as our dogs are.

Our dogs are so conscientious that when eye contact is accidentally made (with one another or with us), they always offer a Calming Signal just to say, "Oops, no fear intended." Even when sleeping, our dogs are so thoughtful, they never line their heads up with another being, as a gesture of peace. This loving action is so benevolent and full of presence. It is truly selfless. On the other side of the coin, a properly socialized dog will apply the Forbidden Angle without hesitation, but only if the situation merits. They will do it tactfully, with the least amount of force necessary. Though dogs are creatures of love and peace, they are completely at ease experiencing fear and using it to communicate.

When it comes to present-moment awareness and emotional intelligence, our dogs seem to have the upper hand on humans. Our thinking minds, driven by the unconscious desires of our ego, create a fog of nonreality that seems to prevent us from being present in our environments. Humans, loving as we may be, are oblivious to what is happening around us because we are stuck in our own heads. We fail to seize our opportunities to make heart-based actions in the now. This unconscious awareness trains our dogs to misbehave, as they misread our emotional cues, angles, and postures as praise or fear for what is happening in the "now," thereby shaping their neuroses and bad behaviors.

In this sense, all of our dog's quirks can be traced back to ourselves without us fully realizing it. Every action we have ever made toward our dog has shaped them into what they are right now. Once we realize this, we become inspired to work on ourselves because we want to improve our dog's temperament.

As you make your way through the case studies found throughout the rest of the book, you will discover that practically everyone is in the same boat. We all have a similar set of ego-based blind spots that inhibit our ability to be a Peaceful Alpha. We are either not aware of how our emotions are miscommunicating to our dogs, or we are not aware of how our dog's emotions are communicating to us. Tapping into the Secret Language of Dogs is not rocket science, though it does take a little practice getting used to in the beginning. Kids and dogs do it all the time without even thinking about it. As you begin to practice the methods your awareness blossoms of its own accord.

Undoubtedly, you will have many of your own Eureka! moments, when you suddenly see how your presence plays a pivotal role in your dog's behavior in any given moment. Your dog truly becomes your guru. The opportunity for improving your dog's temperament (with action and presence alone) inspires you to master yourself. Inevitably, a transformation will begin to take place for both of you. Your dog will become happier, more peaceful, and more attentive to you, and you will begin feeling clearer, calmer, and more energized over time.

# Training Tips
## The Secret Language of Dogs

1. There are three categories of feelings your dog experiences:
   - Pleasant, which reinforces behaviors they're doing right now.
   - Unpleasant, which motivates them to stop doing what they're doing now.
   - Tranquil, the natural vibe they desire, which communicates that everything in this moment is okay.

2. When you give your dog a command, they are paying attention to your emotional energy for communication guidance more than your words. They are tapped into how you feel and what your body is saying.

3. When you call your dog to come, have just a little excitement in your voice and make your posture seem unthreatening. This will make your dog feel confident and motivate it to come quickly to you. Staring at them or having fear in your voice (because they are not listening) motivates them to not want to come back to you.

4. Your Peaceful Alpha power increases the more tranquil you are. The tranquility creates the contrast for the emotions you generate, creating very clear shifts in vibrations your dog can sense with ease.

5. As with any skill, mastering this Secret Language of Dogs takes a little time, but results will start coming in almost immediately.

# Meditation
## Walking with Tranquility

Go for a walk alone along an empty nature trail. Keep your gaze focused on the ground about 10 feet ahead of you. Though you are concentrating on this one point, allow your vision to expand to take in as much as you can see. Remain here for as long as it takes to get comfortable and relaxed in this new sensation. You may enter into a flow-state experience, in which your awareness expands and your talking mind ceases. The simple action of walking mindfully will create the emotional sensation of tranquility. Practice walking like this alone, and once you get comfortable, start taking your dog along for the meditation with you.

Bring your attention to your body and its connection to the earth. With each step you take, kiss the ground with the heels of your feet and roll your weight forward into your toes. Feel the rebound force of gravity rise up in a smooth and balanced way throughout your body. Notice as this energy rises through your legs, into your hips, and up past your belly button. Watch the energy rise into your chest and spill into your open shoulders. Feel your arms loosen and your fingers tingle. Everything remains loose and connected. Observe how the whole body is connected on a string, and reflect on the truth that actions create emotions.

# 3

# Enlightened Dog Training Principles

Silence is praise to the Universe. The more we reflect on our dog's highly sensitive, animalistic, nonverbal consciousness, the better quality relationship we can achieve with them. Ultimately, we'll be able to connect and communicate with them at a much higher level than we imagine possible, sometimes even telepathically.

## Silence Is Golden

In order to illustrate the results we would achieve from doing basic training exercises in silence, let us take a look at Nate and his two-year-old shaggy golden labradoodle Leo. Nate was a grooming client at Woof & Shloof nearly 10 years ago, and he was a masterful Peaceful Alpha.

Our paths crossed every morning at 6:30. I would be sipping coffee at the outdoor cafe, meditating, and gazing at the sun, mentally preparing for my day ahead. Like clockwork, I would see Nate walking Leo down the street, with no leash and an extra-large blue chuckit stick slung over his shoulder. Nate never looked back at his dog, and Leo just followed like an obedient soldier with his tongue flailing out the side of his mouth.

As Nate approached the stoplight near the cafe, he made eye contact with Leo for the first time, preparing him for a strong, silent, assertive command. Using the fetch scepter and the power of touch, Nate silently tapped Leo on the nape of the neck. The dog sat instantly and remained focused for his next command. When the light turned green, Nate clicked his throat. Leo popped up and followed calmly behind his master to the front door of the coffee shop. Nate then whispered something and Leo dropped to his belly, where he stayed with his eyes tethered to the window, loyally awaiting Nate's return.

As I observed this, I reflected on how different Leo was from most of the other dogs I have come across. He was calm, completely attuned to Nate, and unbelievably well-tempered for such a young dog. He was trustworthy, street-smart, and followed his master without hesitation. Nate did not even glance my way as he left the coffee shop. He simply clicked the back of his throat once more and slowly started walking down the sidewalk without looking back. Leo, conditioned by that clicky noise, responded by springing up and following.

Nate masterfully exemplified the enlightened secret that silence speaks. When we are noisy, our dogs, friends, colleagues, and loved ones tune us out. When we are silent, they tune us in. When Nate was leaving the coffee shop, he was able to make a soft clicking noise from the back of his throat and Leo was totally focused on him, despite a gamut of distracting street noises all around him. Leo heard the click and immediately began following his master along the sidewalk. I have no doubt that Nate walked Leo in silence, trained him in silence, and lived with him in silence.

Maintaining a lifestyle of silence gives us superpowers and turns us into masterful Peaceful Alphas. As Nate walked away from his unleashed dog without looking back, he was not walking away blindly. He was deeply listening. His mind's eye saw what his ears were hearing. He heard the dog make a groan as he transitioned from a resting state to an active state. He heard his dog dig its claws into the cement as it began walking. He heard the rhythmic jingle of the metallic tags on Leo's collar. Though Nate was appearing aloof, he remained focused on the sounds his dog was making. From all of these sounds, Nate's mind was able to identify the speed and location of his dog as it trotted behind him, without even looking back.

We might mistakenly think that silence, in a spiritual sense, means the absence of noise. For example, we might believe that our yoga teachers hear absolutely nothing but the blissful silence of the void when they're meditating. This is a total misunderstanding. They hear everything, yet they remain tranquil.

This planet is full of noise, and though we can tune it out, there is no escaping it or the vibrations it makes. Your dog hears everything, just like a meditation master! The wind makes noise. The rain makes noise. Electronics make noise. Our breathing makes noise. As we cultivate a meditative lifestyle, our consciousness begins to evolve. We start hearing sounds without becoming distracted by them. Coincidentally, this is often the very thing that we are trying to train our dog: to not be so reactive to sensations. From a Peaceful Alpha's perspective, silence simply means practicing the skill of nonreactivity to external sounds and inner emotions. Thoughts and feelings, just like sounds, are an endless river of energy. Our relationship to this "noise" defines our energetic vibration to our dog. It also allows us to create that contrast between the regular vibe of tranquility we offer and the emotions we generate from our skillful actions.

As you begin walking your dog in silence, training them in silence, and practice being respectfully silent around them, you will find that your dog begins to tune in to your every move. When you act, they will notice; when you command, they will listen. Your silence will not be misconstrued as an absence of presence. In fact, the opposite is true: silence breeds Peaceful Alpha power.

# The Genius of Repetition

One of the best-kept dog-training secrets I have ever come across is the strategy of lulling your dog into hypnosis using very simple yet predictable sequences, such as "stop" and "go" and "sit" and "down." As you will soon discover, repeatable sequences temper your dog's reactivity, calm their minds, and attune their focus so that it is on you. To me, these characteristics describe the makings of a perfect dog, regardless of their age, breed, or lifestyle.

Let's take a look at an extreme example so you can get an idea of how you could use this technique to calm down your dog, develop Peaceful Alpha power, and release the dog from excessive excitement or anxiety.

I once saw an incredible trainer named David working with a rescued male pitbull who didn't trust humans—this dog had a wildness in his eyes that frightened even me. David tamed him and developed an unbelievable bond with the animal using nothing but two milk crates, a leather leash, and a repeatable sequence.

To set the stage for David, I have to mention that just leashing this dog sent him into a ferocious rage. He snapped, snarled, and lunged at David, hoping his fear-generating actions would keep his new trainer at bay. A true Peaceful Alpha, David displayed a natural loving calmness toward the dog. While other observers questioned the trainer's sanity, I watched in awe as he led the misunderstood beast toward a blue milk crate.

David casually coaxed the large dog to stand up on the cold blue plastic. With nowhere to go, and after roughly 30 seconds of balancing uncomfortably, the pitbull chose to sit down on its own accord. David softly praised the dog as soon as it sat, as if what just happened was no big deal.

In fact, what had just occurred was an incredibly big deal. In the animal kingdom, sitting down communicates a willing act of submission, or emotional surrender. David had cleverly tricked the dog into making a Calming Signal. Where the body goes, the mind follows.

Without saying a word, David led the pitbull off the crate and across the room, where he once more coaxed the dog to stand on a second milk crate. This time, the pitbull sat down much more quickly; hence, the genius of this simple repeatable sequence was already well underway. As they went back and forth from crate to crate over the next several minutes, the dog's mood magically transformed. His fear evaporated. No longer snapping and snarling, the dog grew relaxed, confident, and happy to please his new Peaceful Alpha. In fact, the pitbull started trotting between the crates. Soon, he was beaming with pride and feeling joyful.

Repetition in this fashion lulls the mind into a deep meditative groove of tranquility, allowing us the opportunity to countercondition our dog to the stimulus that triggered them in the first place. Let's say your dog hyper-focuses on squirrels, and you want to reprogram your dog's predatory-based behaviors when they see a squirrel. Simply take them to a park filled with squirrels, ask them to jump onto a park bench, and command them to sit. Once sitting, tell them to jump off the bench and then have them sit once more on the ground.

With the right blend of calm enthusiasm and patience on your part, your dog will become incredibly engaged as they jump up and sit, then jump down and sit. Repeating these simple commands will ignite a desire in your dog to please you almost immediately. In a few moments, the distraction of the squirrels in the background will dissipate because these simple exercises have coaxed the dog's consciousness into a trance-like state. When the mind is calm, the body is also calm. Congratulations, you have just quelled your dog's chase instinct.

This technique doesn't only apply to our dogs; it also applies to humans. Anytime we repeat a predictable sequence with our body, especially with our mind fully engaged in the activity, we experience a profoundly positive shift in our mental, physical, and emotional state.

Be a scientist, and conduct a simple experiment. The next time you have laundry to fold, dishes to put away, or a backyard full of poop that needs to be cleaned, observe what happens when you put your entire mind into the task. Fully surrender to the work. Pay attention to any resistance your ego might have to doing the job.

## The Power of Touch

Touch is a powerful source of connection in any relationship. When a parent puts their loving hand on our shoulder, it has the ability to instantly melt away our worries. Alternatively, when someone points their finger at you, they are making a conflict-seeking action, generating the emotion of fear. This energy easily shuts us down and creates resistance. Peaceful Alphas use the power of touch to consciously communicate with our dogs to shape their behavior. By attuning ourselves to our dog's feelings, we allow our gurus to teach us exactly how to master this enlightened training technique.

Using the power of touch to communicate with our dog requires discernment. We need to know when our hands should make an assertive connection (used to control our dog when their excitement flares) or when we should softly touch our dog (to praise it for carrying out a newly desired behavior). One touch creates fear; the other love. One communicates yes; the other no. One says do more of this behavior; the other says stop it. When our dogs are excited, afraid, or overly stimulated, consciously touching them in an assertive manner mimics how they communicate with one another. In these scenarios, your touch makes wise use of the emotion of fear, because it actually settles their energy by temporarily snapping them out of their emotionally charged state.

On the other hand, mindlessly petting your dog in these moments confuses the message, because it asks them to keep being excited or scared. Though they don't like the feeling of over-excitement, the praise you're giving them inspires them to remain energetically unbalanced because of their strong desire to please you. Remember, we are looking to shape a happy, confident, calm dog in any given situation. Your job as a Peaceful Alpha is to mix both styles of touch to keep your dog's emotions tempered.

To get a better sense of the power of touch and how it can be used as a communication tool with your dog, let us take a look at Figure 5 and study the case of Cuddles's visit to the vet's office.

**Figure 5: Power of Touch**

Gentle touch is always perceived by your dog as loving, praising, and encouraging of present-moment behaviors. Your touch can also be used to command respect, cultivate authority, and discourage unwanted behaviors.

- Touching the nape of the neck is where dogs assert their dominance and discipline one another.
- Hooking your fingers and touching the inner thigh of your dog keeps them anchored to the spot and encourages them to relax.

These places are sensitive to your dog, so make sure you touch them here peacefully (not emotionally charged with e.g. anger or frustration) and with the least amount of force and energy possible. The highlighted places on the diagram have a "snap your dog out of it" effect, and touching them here can be very useful when they are experiencing intense emotions.

Cuddles was a playful three-year-old shiba inu who was boarding in my house while her "parents" were away on an extended holiday. During that time she was due to receive her regular vaccine administration. As we approached the vet's front door, Cuddles dug her heels into the sidewalk and curled her tail under her legs. I sensed her fear and instantly became empathetic to her feelings. Though I did not want us to be late for her appointment, dragging her along the sidewalk seemed both cruel to her and somewhat embarrassing for me. I decided it was a much better use of my energy to tap into the power of touch to communicate that she didn't really have a choice.

I grabbed Cuddles and carried her like a football into the vet's office. The snugness of her body touching mine created a minor calming effect and momentarily relaxed her fright, yet it didn't last long. As I opened the door to the vet's office, I felt her heart rate spike once again. Just being in the waiting room triggered another fit of anxiety in her. While the calm energy from my body touching hers had a soothing effect, it was also an emotional crutch. It was time for Cuddles to grow up and be a big girl.

I sat down in a chair and placed Cuddles on the ground between my feet. Too afraid to see that my legs were offering her a shield of protection, Cuddles instinctually desired to flee the waiting room. Tapping into the power of touch, I softly tugged her scruff backwards, pulling her body into the shield of safety that my legs were offering. The suddenness of my assertive touch sobered her. Instinctually, she knew it was time to surrender, because making contact on the nape of a dog's neck is a familiar connection point communicating status and authority. Cuddles received the intention of my message, which was an order to remain on the ground, between my legs and wait until further notice.

Her body was now shaking as she worked through the undigested, unpleasant feelings that were storming through her mindbody. As her Peaceful Alpha, I wanted to show Cuddles that it's safe right now. When we acknowledge our intense feelings from a place of stillness we can actually experience deep healing, because we allow the pent-up energy to release itself from the body. All too often, our dogs (and we too) want to run away from these buried feelings; however, remaining present with this surge of energy actually allows it to flow out of our bodies. Quite frankly, though the experience is rather intense, it feels euphoric once complete.

Some consider this method a little intense because it forces our dog to go through a momentary unpleasant experience; yet, if you had to choose between a lifetime of your dog being afraid of going to the vet, or a couple minutes of discomfort followed by a release of ancient fear patterning, the choice becomes rather obvious to many of us.

Using my index finger to mimic the sensation of a tooth, I casually applied a downward pressure to the tip of Cuddles' tailbone, encouraging her to sit. When dogs stand, they are only touching the earth with a small amount of their body's surface area. When they sit or lie down, however, more grounding energy from the earth penetrates them with emotional healing and comfort.

It only took a little pressure from my fingertip to coax Cuddles to sit. She let out a big yawn and shook the energy out of her body like a wet duck. Then she gently lay down on her belly, as if asking the earth to take her stress away. Her body shook for a few more seconds and then she surrendered deeply and rested her chin happily on the ground. I was so pleased with her transformation that I spent the next 15 minutes softly petting the top of her skull and massaging her ears. Just when I thought that the situation was under control, fate tempted us once again.

Suddenly, a woman walked in with a frisky little Chihuahua puppy. He looked at Cuddles and instantly went into the down-dog position, growling excitedly. His playful body language gave Cuddles the sense that a play date, right now, seemed like a really awesome idea. The vet's office, in my opinion, is not a place for playful interactions. When dogs are leashed and sharing close quarters, it is highly advisable not to allow their behaviors to escalate beyond a relaxed standing-still position. Any action of play should be discouraged because it sends our dogs the wrong message. There are other patients sharing the waiting room space, and some of them are ill. This is a place of calmness.

Obviously, Cuddles didn't know this expectation yet. Jumping up off her stomach as a response to the Chihuahua's playful invitation, she began wagging her tail feverishly—she was ready to play!

Instinctively, I tapped into the power of touch once again to communicate with her. I gently hooked my fingers on the inside of her back leg, preventing her from moving forward. She was not expecting to feel that sensation, and when she glanced back at me, she was met by my assertive Peaceful Alpha eye contact. There will be absolutely no playing right now, young lady. Stay within the protective boundary of my legs was the message I intended. She blinked, affirming that she understood. I glanced away as a response to her blink, consciously breaking the Forbidden Angle and acknowledging her communication.

This sequence of body language, from both dog and master, offers an example of an effective nonverbal conversation. Our brief chat was over, and we were again on the same page. Now for a word of caution: the belly of a dog is the most vulnerable place to touch them, so we want to be incredibly soft in our touch when we make contact here; too much firmness can startle or hurt them.

Cuddles' experience at the vet's office demonstrates how the power of touch creates calmness. It worked both when she was afraid and when she was excited. Using my hands and a few principles from the Secret Language of Dogs, I was able to alter her emotional responses and improve her behavior, despite the fact that I had no prior relationship with her. When it came time for Cuddles to see the veterinarian, she confidently followed me into the examination room.

# Transformational Effects

Enlightened dog training embodies much more than simply shaping the behaviors our dogs already know how to carry out; it requires an emphasis on the process of training, not necessarily the content. Our dogs already know how to sit, stay, lie down, run, put things in their mouth, drop things from their mouth, wait on a spot, and come. They did all of these for their mother when they were young, and I'm not sure why we think these tricks are so fancy. The results Nate achieved with his dog Leo demonstrate the potential we can all achieve when we incorporate these simple principles on an everyday basis.

# Training Tips
## Teaching Fetch

The game of fetch allows us to play with our dog in a way that taps into their natural desire to wrestle and chase. For this reason, fetch becomes a wonderful way to exercise our dog, allowing us to harness their energy while providing them with a repeatable sequence of commands. Treated this way, fetch becomes a mind-body workout for your dog. Do this in the morning, and discover how calm and disciplined your dog becomes for the remainder of the day.

### Phase 1 – Teaching "Drop It"

1. Use two identical tug toys, such as ropes or squeaky stuffed animals.
2. Keep one behind your back, and begin playing tug.
3. Release the toy from your hand, allowing your dog to take and hold the object freely.
4. Never try to "win" the tug by ripping the toy out of your dog's mouth. We want our dog to feel confident holding the object in their mouth, and we want it to be dropped upon our command.
5. Present the second object from behind your back. Encouraging your dog to play tug with the new toy trains your dog to release the old object, and it will willingly come to you for more fun.
6. Let's name this behavior "drop it."
7. Pick up the original toy, put it behind your back, and continue the game of tug. Repeat these steps, and enjoy playing with your dog.
8. After several rounds of this, and once your dog's natural desire for tugging increases its energy level, ask them to sit or

lie down before you present the toy again. This engages their mind and builds discipline. Give them the toy when they're calm as a reward for their calm temperament. Keep it fun.

Note: Do not move into Phase 2 until you have thoroughly established momentum from Phase 1.

**Phase 2 – Teaching "Bring It"**

1. Play tug with your dog, and cycle the above steps until you get to "drop it."
2. Instead of placing the second toy in your dog's mouth for another round of tug, throw it a few feet away.
3. Encourage your dog to get the toy you just threw.
4. Reward your dog for bringing you the toy by playing tug, which should be easy because they will naturally want to do this.
5. Release your hand from the toy, ask for a "drop it."
6. Repeat this cycle, gradually building up the distance you're throwing the toy.

# Meditation
## Washing the Dishes

We often think of classic meditation as instructions involving stillness, silence, and mindful attention to breathing. For many, the sheer thought of carving out time in our day to practice meditation overwhelms us. The Buddha says that you do not actually need to do this. He taught an entirely different style of meditation for the person who is too busy during the day to find time to meditate the traditional way. Its simplicity is what makes it advanced. He says that any activity is an opportunity for us to deeply immerse our consciousness in the present moment. Let us look at how we can turn the act of washing the dishes as a way to transform ourselves into a Peaceful Alpha.

Allow the dishes to pile up, then immerse yourself in an exercise in the genius of repetition. Turn on some classical music, or work in silence. Stand with your feet shoulder width apart in front of the sink. Consciously sculpt three long smooth breaths in and out of your nose. Pay attention to the space in between the inhale and the exhale, and the gap between the exhale and the inhale. Now breathe naturally, and observe your breath as it finds its own organic rhythm. Approaching any repetitive activity as a meditation allows us to connect with our bodies, tune in to our thoughts, and center ourselves. In this light, we can turn any monotonous chore our egos resist into a meditation that humbles us and brings us internal peace.

Place your hand on the faucet, and feel the temperature of the metal by tapping into the sensation of touch. Gently turn the water on, and put a drain stopper in the sink. Listen to the soothing sound of white noise the flowing water makes as it fills the basin. What temperature is it? What happens in your wrists and arms when the temperature is pleasant versus unpleasant? Be conscious of the total amount of water you use; it's a precious resource.

Mindfully, reach for the dish soap. Squirt an efficient amount into the water, and try to rediscover the childlike, awe-inspiring magic that bubbles exude. Methodically begin scrubbing each dish. Hear the sounds you're making as you scrape food scraps off your plate. Hear the sounds of the swishing, soapy water. Mindfully rinse the plate clean and stack it neatly for drying. As you repeat this cycle, pay attention to the sensation of your hands as they move between air and water. Study the way the water flows off the clean dishes, as if unimpeded by any obstacle. Through the steady practice of meditation, we come to see that we can allow our thoughts to flow freely through us just like water.

As you go through several repetitions of this cycle, take note of your awareness. Has the thinking mind started to subside? Are you naturally attuning to your environment? Can you sense where your dog is in the home? Can you hear any other sounds, such as the air conditioner, the fridge, or the oven? When the scrubbing and rinsing cycle is complete, take a fresh dish towel and methodically dry each item. See if you can put them away without making a sound. Practice the art of not contributing to the external noises within our environment. This is how we train ourselves to appreciate silence, an essential requirement if we want others to tune in to us.

# 4

# Commanding with Respect and Love

One morning I received a frantic call from Grace, a 70-year-old woman who lived alone with her oversized king shepherd Zeus in a 12th-story penthouse apartment in Toronto. Zeus's myriad of problems had spiraled out of control and left Grace feeling helpless and at her wits' end. To make matters worse, guests no longer wanted to come over to her place because her dog would snarl aggressively when they entered the doorway, leaving Grace feeling isolated and anxious.

When Grace walked Zeus outside, he'd lunge at unsuspecting dogs and attract all kinds of negative attention. Elevator rides were particularly traumatizing, because he'd been known to pounce on people in there, too. Recently a child in Grace's building reached out to pet Zeus in the hallway and the dog reacted by frightening the boy and knocking him over. Livid, the mom filed an official complaint with Animal Services. Grace's voice choked up on the phone when she explained that if Zeus had one more incident, Animal Services would force her to surrender him. I said I would be over to help her right away.

Before rushing onto the highway, I took 20 minutes to meditate, with the intention of cultivating my Peaceful Alpha mindset. A Peaceful Alpha is very calm and in tune with their own emotions.

They operate from a place of deep presence and can see things clearly, for what they are. Connected to the moment, they master their body's reactions and consciously use their posture and eye contact to harmonize and uplift the energy of others. Using the Secret Language of Dogs, they generate emotions that shower their pet with the warmth of benevolent leadership, protection, and safety. Like a chivalrous general, a Peaceful Alpha embraces the opportunity to take charge of a situation if need be. Naturally, they do so in a loving and sensitive way.

## Establishing a Peaceful Presence

The first thing I noticed upon arriving at Grace's apartment was the "BEWARE OF DOG" sign posted on her front door. Already detecting my presence from inside, Zeus let out a thunderous bark that echoed down the hallway long before I had a chance to knock. "Get back, Zeusy. Get back, Zeusy," Grace sang fruitlessly, intending to command Zeus away from the door.

Before Grace could open the door, I darted 10 feet down the hall to mitigate any perceived territorial threat I was triggering in Zeus. Suddenly, the door opened, and he burst through the crack, bounding at half-steam toward me.

Grace pretended to act embarrassed. "Zeusy, Zeusy. Stop it," she sang, unconsciously praising his protective behavior for the second time in only a few moments.

I rotated my body 90 degrees to the left and kept my eyes downward with my back resting against the wall. These unmissable Calming Signals communicated my peaceful intentions to Zeus, but would they be enough?

My heart began to thump as Zeus trotted toward me in a straight line. I could feel his eyes studying me. His actions reflected those of assertiveness and dominance. I expected Zeus to keep his eyes down or his head off to the side as a way to avoid eye contact with me. Both would have been classic gestures communicating gentle intentions. While Zeus's conflict-seeking approach scared me, I sensed a loving, unsocialized, and misunderstood soul hiding within.

Before I could think, his mammoth-sized snout started sniffing the crotch of my jeans. I breathed consciously and elongated my exhales to remain calm while being frisked doggy-style. I could already see that the root of Zeus's aggressive behaviors originated from miscommunication and a general lack of socialization. He thought his mom wanted his protection, and he was simply doing his best.

## Our Biggest Blind Spots

Grace led me into the living room and invited me to sit on a couch that was covered liberally in black and golden dog hair. Zeus followed closely behind me and sat on my foot. He seemed relaxed, and was already surrendering to the natural leadership he felt from my peaceful presence, my body language, and my attunement to his Calming Signals. I gently stroked his ear without looking at him, reinforcing the vibe of tranquility. A few moments later, Grace settled across from me and beckoned Zeus to come to her. He loyally obliged.

Grace nervously petted Zeus while recounting her worrisome memories about his elevator lunging, his walking incidents, and the warning she received from Animal Services. Expressing her negative thought-stream stirred up plenty of anxiety within, and made it difficult for Grace to remain present. Zeus, feeling his owner's stress, was now yawning frequently in an attempt to purify the energy. It also occurred to me that he was standing between Grace and me, offering her the Angle of Protection. She was petting him to make herself feel better, yet her soft touch was unconsciously encouraging him to act as her bodyguard.

I interrupted Grace and explained that our emotional energy transfers onto our dogs when we pet them. While it can feel very therapeutic for us to touch them when we feel upset, our emotion simply moves out of us and into them. Karma teaches us that sooner or later we are going to get back what we give (even if we're not aware of the giving part of it). Since energy cannot be created nor destroyed, the burden of temporarily relaxing our own neuroses by petting our dogs unfairly asks them to be our emotional recycling plant.

"Let's give Zeus a break from petting," I suggested. I reminded her that he only lives in the present, and a loving touch reinforces that our dogs should do more of whatever they are doing right now. Zeus misinterpreted Grace's unconscious actions. He was intuiting her touch as praise for protecting her. Once she stopped petting him, the room filled with a deep contemplative silence. The shift in energy had a dramatic influence on her dog's behavior.

Zeus had now repositioned himself so that all of our bodies were connected in the shape of an arc. This friendly and inclusive formation allowed him to feel connected to all of us without making direct eye contact with anyone. Soon his posture shifted from standing, to sitting, to lying down with his head up, to resting with his head on the floor. Zeus was zenning out. Each position served as a Calming Signal that took him into a deeper state of relaxation. He couldn't get any lower to the ground if he tried. Zeus yawned and licked his lips, releasing the last of his built-up stress before thumping his chin on the floor.

I took this moment to point out to Grace that she sang Zeus's name every time she sensed he was going to do something bad: she sang as he guarded her front door, and again as he greeted me in the hallway. I also noted that when we first sat in the living room, Zeus was already calm and relaxed by my foot. To make matters worse, while all of this was occurring, he was standing in front of Grace in a guarding position. The miscommunication was obvious.

Grace had a huge opportunity to change Zeus's behavior simply by changing her own. She had never paid attention to the fact that Zeus always stood in front of her everywhere they went. He stood in front of her in the elevator. He stood in front of her in the apartment. He even walked in front of her. Zeus was controlling all the angles! Grace was starting to understand that if she wanted Zeus to calm down and behave perfectly, she needed to evolve into a Peaceful Alpha, master her angles, and begin praising the right behaviors in the right moments.

## Straight Line Encounters

Almost every client I have ever worked with experienced problematic behaviors with their dogs that was related to at least one of the following: joggers, baby strollers, strangers, other dogs on leash, or traffic. Interestingly, the Secret Language of Dogs provides us with a simple insight and solution to all of these scenarios. This topic is explored further in Figure 6 at the end of this section.

In the animal kingdom, you'll find that both predators and prey are frightened to approach one another in a straight line. They only do it to intentionally seize an asset, act protectively, or seek to discipline, yet from our dog's perspective, the human world has all sorts of unavoidable Straight Line Encounters (SLEs).

Consider regular life—the way humans talk face to face, the way a kid reaches out their hand to pet a dog, or the way you move in a straight line toward your dog when you leash it. These interactions have loving intentions, but our dogs find these unconscious actions scary. While many dogs acclimate themselves to our way of living, we can easily adjust our actions as a way to earn more trust and respect from our furry gurus.

**Figure 6: Straight Line Encounters**

As a general rule, no animal with peaceful intentions would ever approach another animal in a straight line (unless the animal was incredibly unsocialized). In nature, a straight-line motion is a widely known action that generates an intense amount of fear. Dogs will use this on purpose when they want to assert dominance, claim a resource, or discipline another animal.

In the human world, full of sidewalks and hallways, we seem to have paths that are all created in straight lines. No wonder things like skateboards, rollerblades, shopping carts, strollers, and so forth create fear in our dogs when we walk them.

There is, of course, a very simple solution to keeping your dog calm: Stay present, and notice these straight line encounters (SLEs) before your dog does; this should be easy for you to do because you have much better eyesight than your dog. Then place your body in the Angle of Protection, and walk in an arc around the approaching object. We will cover this in more depth later on.

# The Kung Fu Finger

Small spaces, such as elevators, can also trigger fear-based behaviors in our dogs. Recognizing that the option to flee doesn't exist, they use offense, rather than defense, if they become spooked. For this reason, when Grace and I entered the elevator, we placed Zeus in the back corner. Nothing can sneak up on you if your back is in the corner, so this position actually helped make Zeus feel relaxed and safe. Even so, I couldn't trust him yet; he needed to earn that.

Instinctively, I placed what I call my "Kung Fu Finger" gently on the scruff of his neck. When we touch our dogs on the nape of the neck, we remind them that we are the authority. This is where their mother picked them up when they were young and where aggressive dogs target their attacks.

By creating a tooth-like sensation of pressure on his scruff, I communicated to Zeus, *Don't even think about protecting anyone, mister!* My touch was light and peaceful, yet ready to intensify into a gentle squeeze if the situation merited. A lot of habitual stress energy had surfaced when we entered the elevator, and I wanted to recondition Zeus's instinctual protection-based behaviors.

Enjoying his new role as a zenned-out giant, Zeus panted happily and remained seated behind Grace. After completing her first peaceful elevator ride with Zeus since she had adopted him, Grace turned to me and asked, "Can it really be this simple?"

## The Arc: Nature's Line of Peace

In the past, Grace's anxiety about walking Zeus would take her completely out of the moment. Whenever she'd see another dog approaching them, she'd freeze with fear. Under her breath she'd nervously utter, "Don't lunge, Zeusy.  Be good, Zeusy."

Zeus, however, interpreted Grace's behavior as communicating that he should spring into action, her unconscious verbal praise of his name underscoring that she desired his protection detail.

Unaware that she was responsible for manifesting aggressive behavior in her dog, she suggested to me that she needed a two-foot-long leash to feel more in control. Counterintuitively, I suggested instead that if we used a six-foot-long leash we would give Zeus an opportunity to rise to the occasion and earn our trust.

An opportunity soon arose, when, from roughly 100 feet away, I noticed a schnauzer pulling his mindless, cell-phone-talking owner in a straight line toward us.

I asked, "Can you see that dog approaching from far away?"

Grace said, "I wasn't looking, but I do now."

I asked if she thought Zeus would perceive it as a Straight Line Encounter (SLE) threat. She did, and asked "What do we do?"

"Easy. We arc around all SLEs while keeping Zeus on the outside of us," I responded.

Dogs have inferior vision to that of humans, and Zeus had not noticed the SLE approaching us. Using the leash, we led him to the opposite side of us to create an arc pattern.

When Zeus finally detected the schnauzer, he fanned out even farther to the outside, exaggerating his own little arc of communication. Amazingly, he did this naturally! He also licked his lips as he passed the schnauzer, similar to how one motorcyclist waves to another. Zeus understood the peaceful purpose of the arc and appeared much more socialized than we had been giving him credit for. Grace, feeling empowered, could not believe the effectiveness of this simple trick. Check out Figure 7 for more insight on why this little trick delivers so much tranquility.

**Figure 7: The Arc**

Dogs don't move toward one another in a straight line, because they don't want to accidentally create fear in another dog. If you have ever observed dogs off leash, they will always move in circular shapes toward one another. Moving in an arc is an enlightened action, because it creates the emotion of tranquility in dogs.

# Confidence and Communication

Over the next three months, Grace focused on using her posture to communicate with Zeus in a variety of new ways. She stopped petting him unconsciously and became much more relaxed when walking him. Grace had never noticed before that Zeus was such a persistent communicator, and their relationship deepened considerably. She saw that her role as a Peaceful Alpha never ceased.

As she became more present and alert to her environment, Grace's efforts began paying off in more ways than one—no longer feeling like a victim of her circumstances, her newfound confidence in handling Zeus gave her courage when interacting with humans, too. Soon she began speaking assertively and lovingly in all her relationships, as opposed to bottling up her feelings. Able to sense when people became scared, concerned, or not in their body, Grace began to use warmth, kindness, and space to help people to open up and feel comfortable, even when Zeus was not in the picture. The residents in her building who used to scorn her and her "wild dog" began smiling at her. The mother of the boy Zeus had knocked over couldn't help but notice the dramatic improvement with the dog. She and Grace became friends and visited one another's apartments for tea on occasion. Grace never imagined her social life would expand so effortlessly.

# Training Tips
## Commanding with Respect and Love

1. Your posture and mindset determine whether your dog is going to be reactive or at ease. As you earn more of your dog's respect, they will become more calm and trustworthy.

2. Your dog's name has been charged with love since the day you brought them home. Saying their name will reinforce whatever behavior they're doing right now. It is wise to use your dog's name strategically. Try saying it when they are doing something positive or when you want them to come to you. Never use it when they are doing something bad, because they will think you want them to continue doing the undesired behavior.

3. When petting a dog, you are pouring your emotions through your hands. If you only pet your dog when both of you are feeling calm, you may not have many training issues to correct later. "Dog friendly" people are often perceived as threatening Straight Line Encounters (SLEs) by your dog. They approach in a straight line, are loud, and reach out their hands to say hello. To your dog, this is a sequence of increasing threats, making the person not very friendly at all.

    Eliminate lunging by walking your dog in an arc past any triggers. When dogs are leashed, they might lunge as an instinctual fearful reaction to an SLE. If they were not leashed, their instinct would be to make an arc around the SLE and continue forward.

# Meditation
## Cultivating Your Eagle Eye

Start this meditation sitting on a park bench with your foot on your dog's leash and your hands resting naturally in your lap. Feel your feet on the earth. Allow the weight of your core to melt into the bench. Stay here until you feel your attention centered in your body. Develop a feel for your dog. What posture is it in? Tune in to its rate of breathing. Keep a fraction of your awareness tethered to your furry guru's Calming Signals as you meditate.

With your eyes open but your eyelids half-closed, softly gaze in the direction of the incoming flow of traffic. Focus gently on something that is six feet away, and stay there for 10 breaths. Next, let your eyes find another focal point 12 feet away, and hold your soft gaze for another 10 breaths. You're already viewing things beyond your dog's range of sight. Repeat this pattern every 10 breaths, as you extend your focal point farther and farther until you reach your limit.

Now reverse the pattern, and bring your focal point gradually closer to the starting point. Do this cycle once, or repeat it several times. How was your vision changed? Has your dog made any subtle shifts to its posture? Can you link any of the Calming Signals your dog makes to stimuli coming from the present environment?

# 5

# Power Objects
## The Solution to Your Dog's Embarrassing Behaviors

What do the smell of a bacon sandwich wafting from the coffee table, the crinkle of a random piece of plastic (that sounds like a treat bag), or the *ding* of your doorbell have in common? These sensual stimulations instantly activate excitement in your guru's nervous system. In these precise moments, when your dog experiences strong feelings, your commands will most certainly fall on deaf ears. Welcome to the concept of Power Objects.

At a neurological level, familiar stimuli create waves of conditioned excitement (or fear) in our dogs. As we have come to see, a gamut of embarrassing behaviors, such as jumping, excessive barking, ankle biting, whining, or occasional aggression, always accompany these intense emotions.

While power objects are the root of many of our dog's behavioral issues, they also come with an elegant and effortless solution baked within. By mimicking the body language of an alpha dog as they seize assets or guard territory, we can counter-condition our dog's excitement to any power object both quickly and calmly by leveraging a very simple law in the animal kingdom: the top dog always eats first, claims the asset with ease, and chooses the best resting spot with grace. No gorilla dares challenge the silverback's authority, because the troop adores him and respects him deeply. If you are ready to acquire this level of status with your dog, this chapter offers you a roadmap to achieving it.

The resource-guarding technique we will explore asks you to increase the intensity of your "alpha" vibe while simultaneously remaining dialed into the "peaceful" vibe. Once you begin to see how calmly your furry guru responds to your gentle authority, a newfound confidence will naturally emerge within you. Your emotional intelligence will increase, and so will your communication skills with people, especially those who are easily excitable (or quick to anger).

## Earning Top-Dog Status

When a wolf hunt comes to an end, no pack member dares to show excitement around the spoils, nor do they even think about eating before the alpha male and female of the pack. In fact, we will often see the alphas assert ownership over the family meal before they even take a bite. While this is happening, the rest of the wolves will calmly fan away and become still (either standing, sitting, or lying down) while they patiently await a cue from their respected leaders to partake of the game.

In my dog daycare, I noticed this to be true with dogs as well.

Imagine having this kind of status with your dog. In a nutshell, it means that you can accidentally (or on purpose) drop a fresh slice of pizza on the floor and your dog won't even dream about going for it. When you have top-dog status, your dog will back away from the pizza, look to you for acknowledgment, then lie down and ready itself for another nap, as if nothing exciting just happened.

If you feel any resistance when reading this statement, because you just "know that your dog would never do that," you are in for a pleasant surprise. I encourage you to open your mind; earning top-dog status might just be a whole lot easier than you think.

Try this little experiment. With your dog in the kitchen, micro-wave a hot dog, and place a reasonably sized chunk of it in their bowl, but do not put it on the floor. Slowly begin walking around the perimeter of your kitchen holding this irresistible lure near your body. Do not talk to your dog nor encourage any specific behaviors. Just observe them quietly out of the corner of your eye while you move. The invisible scent trail wafting in your wake becomes the power object. If your dog approaches you and starts jumping up excitedly, react with the aloofness of a Peaceful Alpha, and they will gently calm down. Accomplish this by turning your back on your dog, and begin walking in the other direction. Remember, this action is used to create the emotion of tranquility.

Stay present, and check in. Is your dog offering you space as a way of communicating respect, or are they hawking you opportunistically, waiting for your attention to slip so that they can steal the hot dog? The more space they offer you, the more you can trust them. The depth of calmness your dog is experiencing during this exercise is in direct relationship to how much respect they have for your Peaceful Alpha authority. The key to earning more respect is to remain calm, patient, and nonreactive. That is the main point of this exercise. Continue circling the room while holding the bowl.

The next iteration of this exercise is to test out your alpha status. Every now and then, simply stop and square your body up to your dog. Stare briefly into your dog's eyes, and observe what he does. These subtle conflict-seeking gestures you have just made, along with the fact that you're holding a power object, are primal actions as far as your dog is concerned. They should respond to your assertive communications by immediately offering you a variety of lip-licks, yawns, or raised paws to communicate their non-challenging (peaceful) intentions. Right now, you are testing your dog in a big way. Do not look away until your dog looks away, and surely, they will. As soon as that happens, turn your gaze away to create tranquility, and continue circling the room for a few more minutes.

Leveraging the immense power of the Forbidden Angle, and the momentum you have been accumulating thus far, you are now going to intensify the training session. With calmness and attunement to your dog's emotions, turn directly toward them once more, stare with a modest level of intensity, and make an authoritative sound. This sound will become your "chill out" command later, so play around with it, and use any noise that comes naturally to you (such as a snap of your fingers, a stomp of your foot, or a sharp "NO!" with your deep voice).

As a result of your intensified actions, your dog will retreat. Then place the bowl on the floor between your feet. This is the Asset Ownership position. Animals claim resources from one another by maneuvering over them or closer to them and issuing a challenging stare. Your dog will know what to do next. In typical guru fashion, observe the master as they surrender fully.

# Controlling the Resources to Control the Energy

You have just begun the art of commanding your dog to enter a state of meditation. Trust the process. Be patient, and remain in the asset-guarding position because the fun part of the training session has only just begun. Now that you have established ownership over the object your dog desires, they will not attempt to snatch it unless you lose focus and become distracted. Observe your dog over the next 10 minutes or so as its attention becomes single-pointed on the hot dog (the object of their meditation). Notice as your dog progresses through increasingly relaxed positions, organically searching for stillness in their body.

If your dog is standing, they will soon sit, lie down, and eventually rest their chin on the floor. Please memorize this sequence. I refer to it as the Sequence of Surrender and cover it in a little more depth in Figure 8. This is typically when they will audibly yawn or snort a nasally grunt notifying you of their deep surrender. Soon, they will become blissfully relaxed (possibly in a small pile of their own drool), yet will maintain a deep state of alert-tranquility like the meditation master they are. When you finally arrive at this destination, reward your furry guru calmly, giving them a chunk of hot dog, and walk away like an alpha, as if nothing unusual just happened.

**Figure 8: Sequence of Surrender**

We can tell a lot about how our dog is feeling (mentally and emotionally) by their posture. This is especially true when we have placed a limit on their behavior (such as tying them to a post or guarding a power object they desire). At first, the dog will experience strong emotions (or resistance). This is reflected in the standing-up position. As they begin to surrender, they will always go through the same three predictable postures: they will sit, then lie down, then fully rest their chin on the floor.

Stay calm, and patiently wait for the entire sequence to unfold. In each position, the dog is actually putting more surface area of his body on the earth. Your furry guru is literally grounding their energy into a deep state of relaxation. A wise Peaceful Alpha memorizes this sequence and only rewards their pet when they have reached the depths of surrender.

Congratulations, you have just turbo-charged your Peaceful Alpha status. You have also taught your dog that you love them when they respond to your authority by lying down and being calm.

Your newly developed resource-guarding technique (or "chill out" command) now becomes a versatile communication tool and can be applied creatively in a variety of ways that you can experiment with.

For example, when your dog snatches a dirty sock from your laundry for a game of tug, make your assertive noise, march toward them in a straight line, and watch as they drop the sock and offer you a Calming Signal. Or when your dog charges the door because you just received a package from Amazon, clap your hands and walk with purpose toward your dog. When they retreat, square your back to the doorway and claim it as your territory. Stare at your dog and tell them no, then watch them surrender before you turn the handle. Claiming authority over everyday Power Objects will bring a great sense of peace and gentleness to your dog's disposition and to your home. Figures 9 and 10 will shine more light on the nuances of these postures and their effects.

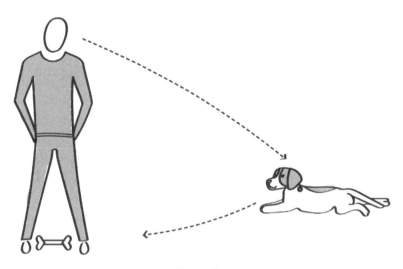

**Figure 9:**
**Asset-Guarding Position**

One of the fastest ways to calm your dog down, earn their respect, and temper their emotions is to introduce a power object into the equation, then claim it as your own. Standing with your feet directly on the object your dog desires while staring at them sends a very clear message: This is mine! Since the Asset-Guarding position is well known to the animal kingdom, your dog will remain focused on the power object (and you) but will begin to surrender to your natural role as leader.

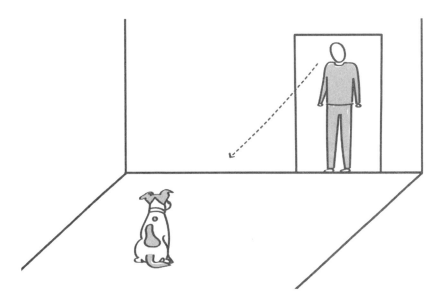

**Figure 10: Territory-Guarding Position**

The crack of the open front door (or any enclosure) represents the access point to your territory. You may have noticed that your dog always runs to this place and sneaks in front of you. The next time you open your door, take a moment to claim the territory as yours. Position yourself between the crack of the door and your dog. Make direct eye contact with your dog, and stare at them until they retreat. They will naturally move away and begin communicating with you using Calming Signals. Wait until they sit or lie down of their own accord and then praise them.

# The Healthy Side of Fear

We need to let go of the idea of training dogs in the traditional way. All animals know that they need to behave calmly and respectfully when their leader guards a territory or an asset. The female alpha wolf doesn't have to train her pups; she knows they are capable of remaining calm in her presence, and she expects it at all times. Challenging your dog over a chunk of hot dog might feel really intense, awkward, or scary to you, but your furry guru knows exactly how to respond.

We are the ones who need the training. Specifically, we need to cultivate our inner stoic when our emotions boil up. Many humans avoid conflict, but what we are really avoiding is feeling the fear these situations generate in us. Practicing this little confrontation with your dog actually helps transform your inner alchemy, making you feel more comfortable and confident with your own fear.

We definitely do not want our dogs to fear us, but we do want our dogs to respect our leadership, especially when we are establishing rules around resources and territory. By staying open to your dog's Calming Signals, you learn when you're being too scary. Your compassion for your dog will motivate you to find softer ways to generate this expression of power.

## Transformational Effects

Peaceful Alphas are in the business of living in a continuous state of presence so that we can help balance the energies of our dogs as well as our environments. In order to be able to do this we must find a way to balance our own energies first.

When we encounter strong emotions like fear and anxiety, humans unconsciously tend to turn to distractions like social media, television, sweets, or bad habits. In this chapter, you were asked to bring mindfulness to your posture and alertness to your focus as you engaged in resource-guarding encounters with your dog.  For many of us, these actions stir up intense resistance within us, similar to the sensation of anxiety or fear. Simply practicing this exercise with your dog provides you with opportunities to find comfort in the discomfort of the now. When we resource-guard with our dogs, they surrender to conditions in the present moment immediately. If they can do it, why can't we?

# Training Tips
## Power Objects

1. The proximity of your dog in relation to the power object you have seized represents the level of respect they have for your status. The farther away they are, the more they respect your authority.

2. Use eye contact and other assertive gestures while you relate to the power object, using the Resource Guarding posture. Instinctively, your dog will start to become calm and submissive.

3. Walking away from a power object after displaying ownership is your way of communicating that you no longer own it. Unless you guard it, your dog will think it's free for the taking.

4. Presence is power. When we're distracted, or engaged in our habits, our dogs look to our body language (which often makes us appear as being aloof). They take this non-action as us giving them consent to continue doing whatever they were doing.

# Meditation

## Power Object Training

Place a chair beside the cabinet in which you store your dog's kibble. Sit comfortably, and feel your weight sink into the connection points that make contact with the ground. Feel your feet placed beneath your knees. Imagine that you're drawing red power through the earth, up your legs, into the base of your pelvis. Imagine that it accumulates there and pools in your belly. Notice your breathing rhythm, and allow it to flow at an organic pace.

Begin to imagine that you're a lion, an animal no dog would dare challenge. Slowly stand up, and remain still; this is known as Mountain Pose in yoga. Softly gaze at your dog, sending it the tiniest vibration of fear and inviting it for a challenge. Nonchalantly gaze away when you see a Calming Signal, then slowly open the cabinet door. Quietly scoop some kibble into the bowl. Turn and face your dog, neither moving forward nor backward. Standing your ground and breathing, you invite another challenge by making direct eye contact, while simultaneously communicating that this resource is yours.

Pay close attention to how you feel. The conflict-seeking gesture tends to bubble up the energy of fear into our auras as we do this. Breathe with it. Don't react. Give yourself the chance to digest your own emotions, and this will result in deep internal peace. Stay viscerally present, while remaining still and relaxed. Wait patiently until your dog exhibits their natural Calming Signals, then place the bowl between your feet, the natural posture for ownership.

When your dog's body begins to settle into the earth, go back to your chair and meditate, this time focusing on the bowl of kibble. Do this for 10 minutes, then walk away without looking back, giving consent for your dog to eat it. Alternatively, you may offer the bowl to your dog by pushing it toward them. Slowly walk away—the meditation is over.

# 6

# Crate Training
## Meditation Chambers for Your Canine

Several years ago, Brian and Ashanti fell in love while working together as physiotherapists in a healing center in Atlanta, Georgia. While on their honeymoon in Thailand, the spiritual couple adopted a shaggy street mutt they named Buddha. Street-smart, he walked beside them on the leash, never barked, never got excited around other dogs, and needed no extra training.

But with the arrival of the couple's newborn son, things dramatically changed for the worse. Their dog took up the habit of chronically scratching his neck, to the point where it became raw. Worse, Buddha started pooping in the kitchen in the evenings, despite an exhausted Brian taking him for extra walks. He also started whining an obnoxiously high-pitched screech every time the baby cried, which was basically all day long.

Brian and Ashanti grew concerned that they did not have the time nor the energy to invest in training their beloved dog, and they were becoming haunted by thoughts that they would have to give him up for adoption. Luckily, I had the perfect solution for this conscientious, free-spirited couple, but whether they would buy into its simplicity and its efficacy, I could not yet be certain.

## We All Need Our Own Room

Buddha used to sleep in the couple's bedroom at night, rest in their yoga studio in the morning (which was now the baby's nursery), and stay close to them as they migrated throughout their house during the day. Since the arrival of the newborn, however, they failed to notice that their dog suddenly became displaced in his own home. What they did notice was that he started self-isolating in the basement, burrowing himself beneath the sofa in the guest suite, and lying under an antique sewing machine in the living room.

Ashanti felt sorry for Buddha. She missed the constant comfort and connection of his formerly tranquil presence, an energy she had not fully realized she depended on to help her mood. Dogs are sensitive to our emotional vibration. They detect the significant difference in flow when we are feeling loving affection and when we are feeling sadness. They interpret both emotional broadcasts as present-moment guidelines for their expected behavior. Since the latter neither falls into the "love" nor the "tranquil" bucket of communication reinforcers, one could expect Buddha to be a little confused, frustrated, and stressed out.

Though these seemed like significant issues to Brian and Ashanti, I explained that there was really nothing serious happening here. Buddha needed some help processing the fact that the yoga room was becoming a nursery, and that the overall energy of his environment would never be the same again. Luckily, because of their deep connection with the present moment, our dogs adapt much faster to changing environments than humans expect. In short, their furry guru simply needed a little quiet space, structure, and solitude so that he could recharge his emotional battery.

## Why We Should Crate Dogs

Practically every human I have ever worked with is biased against the idea of crating their dog, Brian and Ashanti included.

Figure 11, at the end of this section, is meant to be a subtle trick. Crates tend to look like prisons. But what if they didn't? How would you feel about them? While owners worry about placing a doggie prison in their kitchens, from a behavioral standpoint, I question the wisdom behind giving our dog free rein in the house. Frankly, the lack of structure feels completely unnatural to dogs and invariably exacerbates their anxiety. In nature, wolf and fox pups and other den animals are born and raised in sheltered lairs, such as caves or tree holes. While their mothers use these locations to protect their babies from predatory animals and shield them from the elements, they also serve another underrated purpose, to which your dog will attest, if you give them the chance.

These animals come to associate their dens as emotional sanctuaries. Domestic dogs are not born in dens, but their instinctual responses (once they adopt their crate) suggest that they know exactly what to do in them: to go there for reprieve, surrender, and relaxation. This is why professional working dogs (bomb sniffers, police, search and rescue, and special needs) all spend time in their crate each day. The handlers do this to ensure that their canines are calm and emotionally restored so that they can perform their jobs. If the professionals do it, why would it be bad for a household dog like Buddha?

**Figure 11: Dog Sanctuary**

We humans tend to unconsciously resist the idea of putting our dog in a crate, feeling that by so doing we are imprisoning them.

# Accelerating the Crate Adoption Phase

When I arrived at Brian and Ashanti's apartment, it was obvious to me (and Buddha) that the perfect place for his new crate should be where the antique sewing machine was situated. He already spent a significant amount of time there, because it provided a glimpse of the entire room, the hallway, and the front door. While Brian and Ashanti thought he was "divorcing" them, he was actually remaining incredibly connected. The sewing machine offered Buddha the illusion of denlike protection. He was clearly going under there of his own accord to soothe his nerves. For these reasons, Brian and Ashanti agreed that crating might offer a simple solution to their problems.

We cleaned off Buddha's travel crate, covered it with old yoga blankets, and placed it where the sewing machine collected dust. I asked if I could use a high-value treat, like a hunk of cheese, to help accelerate the crate adoption process. Without saying a word to Buddha, I walked over to his open-doored den, threw a sizable morsel inside, and calmly said "go to bed." The lure of the cheese was irresistible, and Buddha instantly trotted over to the crate. As he stuck his nose inside, I gently nudged him, saying "good boy," until he waddled calmly inside.

Buddha trusted me and felt no fear about entering the crate, which meant that this first training exercise was successful. Further conditioning repetitions followed the first in rapid succession, each exercise building on the one before.

A few minutes later, I took another morsel of cheese and said "go to bed" again. Just like the first time, I tossed the lure into the crate, only now I had different expectations, and they were going to be steep.

When we initially teach a command to our dogs, remember that we are really just shaping a specific behavior so that we can name it later. Just like he did the first time, Buddha trotted to the crate, only during this iteration he decided to go all the way inside to fetch the cheese of his own accord. I acknowledged this moment by saying "good boy," then I shut the door behind him. He was a little surprised when he turned around to see that he could not come out when he wanted, but that is perfectly fine. Peaceful Alphas are conscientious commanders. We don't ask our dogs to do things; we tell them to do things. They listen to us and serve us with joy, because our actions emanate love in all forms.

Often the biggest mistake we make while we await our dog's initial moment of surrender in the crate is that we unconsciously stare at them or hover around the door so we can see what's going on inside. We forget this action is an expression of the Forbidden Angle; it suggests to our dogs that they are doing something wrong or should be afraid of us right now.

For this reason, I stepped to the side, turned my back to Buddha, and sat on the floor beside the gate while pretending to be aloof. He perceived my actions as Calming Signals, communicating that it was okay for him to relax. A few moments later, I heard Buddha let out a long sigh as his belly, chest, and chin softly thumped their way down to the earth.

Perhaps counterintuitively, I rewarded this behavior by opening the gate and giving him the freedom to leave anytime he chose. In a soft and loving voice, I told him he was a good boy, then I stood up and walked away like an alpha (without looking back). Interestingly, he was in no rush to get up and leave.

We repeated this little routine many times during the remainder of the session. We made it fun, yet were careful not to get too excited once he started associating "go to bed" with lying down in the crate, particularly because we wanted him to remain calm. By the end of the session, Buddha had the foundation for an amazing new command. He knew to go to his sanctuary every time we said "go to bed," and he knew to lie down in it. My clients wondered how this was going to fix his relationship with the baby, and whether it would stop him from pooping in the kitchen, but they trusted the process.

They committed to working on this routine with Buddha for a week, gradually increasing the time he spent in the crate to longer periods, both with them in the room and on his own while they were upstairs with the baby. When they crated him for longer durations, I encouraged them to give a high-value chew like a stuffed KONG or a raw hide to distract him while he was alone. Once he was sated from chewing, he would drift off into a pleasant meditation followed by a nap.

I suspected that he would adopt this crate as his new refuge and that all his behavioral problems would inevitably resolve themselves on their own.

## Recharging the Emotional Battery

It was not that Buddha wasn't happy with the baby, nor that he couldn't peacefully coexist with the new family unit. Rather, he wasn't happy with the sudden influx of "unpleasant" energy that he was feeling in his environment. The constant crying of the baby, the newly detectable stress in his parents, the disruption to the household rhythm—these were the reasons why he was pooping in the kitchen and waking up the neighbors with his supersonic howling. These stress-relieving reactions were simply undesirable behavioral outbursts that could no longer be contained in his body. Buddha's emotional battery had run dry and desperately needed to be "plugged in" again to recharge.

Dogs covet their own safe resting place in our home, yet we often fail to provide it for them. Why else would they seek refuge under a couch during a thunderstorm, cower under the kitchen table when our buddies come over to watch football, or in Buddha's case, hide under the sewing machine when the baby cries. If your dog is crate trained, it will go in there many times throughout the day of their own accord. It offers them privacy, while allowing them to still feel connected to the family.

# The Transformation

I spoke to Ashanti on the phone just two weeks after our session. She and Brian had kept up with the "go to bed" routine, and unsurprisingly, Buddha was now going into the crate of his own free will many times throughout the day. Ashanti said that he loved it, and that he was considerably calmer when the baby cried now. This made her and Brian really happy.

She also noticed that Buddha had stopped randomly scratching his ear and the rawness on his skin had healed over. She could not believe that she had not noticed how stressed he was before. Importantly, he stopped pooping in the kitchen at night, and when she commands him to "go to bed," he literally trots into the crate and lies down, waiting for a piece of cheese.

With exuberance in her voice, she said, "I know we are not punishing him if we send him into it. I genuinely know that he feels happy and safe in there. He even goes in there on his own when the baby cries."

Crating Buddha reminded Ashanti about the power of meditation, and that she had let her own practice slip when the baby arrived. Perhaps because of the stress that change creates, we tend to think we never have enough time to meditate, yet that is precisely why we need it. Ashanti was grateful to get her practice back on track.

"Even as a seasoned meditator, I sometimes forget how much clarity and peacefulness it gives me," she said. "It makes me a better wife, mother, and dog owner. It even gives me the feeling that I have more time, because I'm much more conscious of how I spend my energy." She was a total Peaceful Alpha.

# Training Tips
## Crate Training

1. Select a strategic location for your crate. Place it somewhere that provides an excellent view of the house. You want your dog to feel connected to the family while it is crated. Perhaps they already have a special spot you can leverage.

2. Make it a cozy place for your dog. Cover it with a blanket that has your scent on it. Put something comfortable on the floor for it to rest on.

3. The crate should be large enough for your dog to stand, turn around, and lie down comfortably.

4. Bowls of water in the crate are not the greatest idea. Giving your dog water before crating them, followed by a pee break and more water after crating, eliminates the risk of urinating in the crate because of a full bladder.

5. Every time you put your dog in the crate, give them a command they will recognize, such as "go to bed."

6. Feed your dog all of its meals in the crate so that they have a positive association with the crate and to accelerate the adoption phase.

7. Give your dog high-value chews, such as stuffed KONGs, or bully sticks, in the crate, for the same reason as above.

8. Remain in the room with your dog while they are adopting the crate. Your calm presence helps them find comfort. Once your dog surrenders, begin leaving the room and coming back. Never take your dog out of the crate when they are excited.

Only let them out when they are calm. Note: Opening the door reinforces whatever emotional state your dog is currently in.

9. A three-month-old puppy can stay in the crate for up to one hour during the day without soiling themself. For every month in age, add one more hour. Adult dogs can easily spend over eight hours in the crate, but be cautious about crating them for too long.

Note: Do not crate your dog during the day if you crate them at night.

# Meditation
## Clearing Stress

Allow your body to relax into a comfortable position. Begin to scan all of the parts of your body, starting with your toes and working your way up to the top of your skull. Pay attention to your breath, allowing it to flow freely and resisting the need to sculpt it. Perhaps your breathing feels a little jagged and shallow, or perhaps it is long and smooth. As you linger in this step, discover what's going on with your breath, your life force, and allow it to nourish you. Using your imagination, make an egg-sized bubble shape of purple energy behind your eyes. This is the command control center of your body, and with deep concentration and imagination, we can use it to influence our energy.

Command your lungs to smooth out your breath and deepen their intake. Imagine that you see them shifting gears, bringing fresh oxygen into your solar plexus, the center where your energetic battery lives. Begin to imagine white light spreading its way up your spine, past your heart center, through your throat, and into the crown of your head. This light is cleansing you from any stress related to the past or future. Remain here for as long as you like.

As you tune into feeling the organic pulse of your breath in your body more deeply, become viscerally present to your senses. See your thoughts floating past you. Feel sensations in the body coming and going. Hear the noises in the background, but don't let them stick. Allow this meditation to recharge your battery so that you can reenter your life with calmness and presence.

# 7

# Healing Neuroses and Anxiety

Fred and Sonia lived in a beautiful four-bedroom house in the sub-
urbs of Vancouver, British Columbia. The youngest of their three
children recently moved out to attend university, creating an intol-
erable vacuum of silence in their home. The empty-nesters decided
to fill the void by adopting Bon Jovi, a middle-aged chocolate lab.

They anticipated that Bon Jovi would be calm and easy because
of the myth that age and breed are successful indicators of a calm
temperament in a dog. In my experience, lifestyle, environment,
and leadership make for much better predictors.

Within a few days of his arrival, Bon Jovi had already licked all of
his toes red, a classic expression of anxiety in dogs, similar to how
children bite their nails. This peculiar behavior had gone unnoticed
by Fred and Sonia, however, as the main reason they had reached
out to me was to cure Bon Jovi's problematic flight instinct. He had
already escaped through the couple's front door so many times
that Sonia had stitched a GPS tracker into his fluorescent collar.
Recently, the not-so-street-smart dog ran across the highway, and
nearly got himself hit by a car several miles down the road.

Thanksgiving weekend was just three days away, and the couple
expected to host a massive dinner for family and friends. Now,
Fred and Sonia were incredibly frightened for the safety of their
new dog, and all Sonia could think about was that the front door
would be opening up to 20 times that evening. If Bon Jovi did

not escape, he would certainly whine, howl, and make a huge fuss every time the doorbell rang. The thought of locking him in the bedroom or tying him outside held very little appeal for her. She wanted a calm dog she could trust and did not want to deal with his stress-based behaviors anymore.

## The Curse of Undigested Emotions

Seated at Sonia's kitchen table enjoying some tea, I explained to her that wild animals always operate with a deep and persistent sense of calmness and mental clarity; whereas, the opposite seems to be the case for many domestic dogs and their human beings. In the heat of intense anxiety we lose clarity, as we are overtaken by a surge of unpleasant emotions—all connected to past or future (not present)—leading to unconscious destructive thought and behavioral patterns. The energy of undigested traumatic experiences is alive and wants to be acknowledged, felt, and processed. When we allow this flood of old feelings to flow through our conscious awareness, we find healing, peace, and tranquility.

Humans are equally susceptible to acting out our neuroses, just like our dogs. Sonia was no exception. Even when Bon Jovi was contained inside the home, she would constantly worry about his next escape. As she worried, she intensely paced the narrow hallway, walking past Bon Jovi in an SLE (straight line encounter) as many as 10 times since I had arrived. Though her intentions were harmless, it created a conflict-seeking emotion. Unfortunately, this resulted in a neurotic dog becoming even more neurotic.

As I was explaining this to Sonia, a soft thud occurred outside the front door from a package being dropped off. Bon Jovi's instinct kicked into overdrive, and his overgrown claws dug deep scratches into the wooden floor, practically churning to sawdust as he sprinted to the crack of the front door. Sonia looked at me with exasperation as he jumped and barked at the door.

# The Alpha Guards the Territory

From the moment we bring a dog into our home, they expect us to behave like an alpha. To be frank, most of our dogs feel insecure in their own homes 100 percent of the time. Their keen sense of awareness constantly detects motion around the doors, windows, and fences (which to them are portals into our territory). Since domestic dogs do not understand that humans use locks, alarms, and police protection for this, they judge the safety of their situation based on their observations of what they perceive as mindless behaviors on our part, such as remaining glued to our iPads while the threat of the neighbor's Yorkshire terrier walks by. If we ignore what they perceive as a threat to their territory, this only further stresses our dogs. A dog may have incredible senses, but they see the human as head of security, so in their eyes, we seem to be demonstrating aloofness at the wrong time.

The access points to our home are, in fact, power objects for our dog, and we can control the energy of our dogs by seizing control of the territory; therefore, if we claim the door, the fence, or the bay window using the asset-guarding position, our dogs will instantly retreat and begin to surrender.

Bon Jovi needed Sonia to notice the imposing threats that the mailman, guests, and neighbors posed from his point of view. Unfortunately for him, anytime the doorbell rang, Sonia feared and obsessed over thoughts of her dog racing out the crack of the door. She was literally frozen in her own fright, preventing her from exhibiting that Peaceful Alpha presence her dog required.

# Calming a Neurotic Mind

As a reminder, Power Objects are the source of most of our dog's emotional reactivity, and are also the solution. Remember, from the experiment with the hot dog, when we relate to power objects as a Peaceful Alpha, by using the Forbidden Angle to resource-guard it, our dogs behave in a predictable and submissive way. First they sit, then they lie down, then they rest their chin on the earth and begin meditating. Though their bodies are deeply relaxed, their minds remain calm and alert, allowing them to focus on us, the "owner" of the power object at hand.

Wasting no time with my new client, I got right down to business. Fred and Sonia informed me that barbecue salmon was Bon Jovi's favorite snack, telling me that he salivated every time they took some out of the fridge. Armed with this knowledge, I asked Sonia to put an entire leftover filet of the high-value power object into Bon Jovi's dog bowl, then slowly walk with the bowl in her hand down the hallway, stopping approximately 15 feet from the front door.

The scent trail was a potent lure for Bon Jovi. He trotted after us and stopped when we stopped, at the edge of the stairs facing the entrance. Bon Jovi would now perceive these stairs as a natural territorial boundary, so we leveraged this to shape some new behavioral patterns. Rather than Bon Jovi escaping out the front door when the bell rang, we were going to train him to lie down on this spot and calmly focus on Sonia, regardless of what happened around him. The distance of 15 feet from the doorway acted as an insurance policy, creating a nice buffer of space for Sonia to operate and greet guests when they arrived.

## Down and Stay: The Peaceful Alpha Way

I asked Sonia to place the bowl of salmon at the top of the stairs and enter the asset-guarding posture (placing it between her feet). Making direct eye contact with Bon Jovi, Sonia leveraged the fear-inducing vibe that the Forbidden Angle generates, communicating that the salmon was hers, the Alpha's. Bon Jovi's focus became one-pointed on the high-value treat and his mind-body began surrendering. He offered a variety of Calming Signals to Sonia—

yawning, lip-licking, and looking downward—communicating that his energy was relaxing. He was clearly no threat to the resource she was guarding. I reminded Sonia to exercise patience and non-reactivity (two virtues of a true Alpha) to encourage Bon Jovi to settle down more quickly, and he transitioned into the predictable lying-down, chin-down position within minutes.

Observing Bon Jovi's breathing pattern, we watched as it shifted from an excited stage (huffing and puffing) into a gentle, almost imperceptible rise and fall in his chest. I am always blown away at how quickly and effortlessly dogs can surrender to the Alpha. Here lay this furry guru, 15 feet from the door, experiencing a blissful state of awareness, focused entirely on his master. We gave him a couple chunks of salmon, communicating that we wanted him to continue to lie down.

## Guarding the Line:
## Controlling Power Objects at Distance

Often, when we move away from an asset, we do not think to continue guarding it with our body language. We must be cautious of this, because our dog will sense this moment as an opportunity to snatch the power object—aside from us losing our Peaceful Alpha power, our dog has effectively decided to break out of their "down-stay" position before we release them.

For the purpose of this training exercise, I wanted to teach Bon Jovi to lie down at the top of the stairs in front of the bowl of salmon and stay there, even as Sonia moved around and introduced a variety of potentially triggering stimuli.

The concept of guarding the line is an advanced way to communicate Asset Ownership over a power object from a distance. Take a peek at Figure 12 to get a feel for what the body posture and nonverbal communication looks like. When we implement this technique correctly, our dog naturally remains anchored to their spot and focused on you, enabling you to walk away while your dog remains motionless in front of the power object you were initially guarding. This technique offers you an incredibly efficient tool for shaping your dog into a reliable "down-stay" position and can be applied in a variety of creative ways.

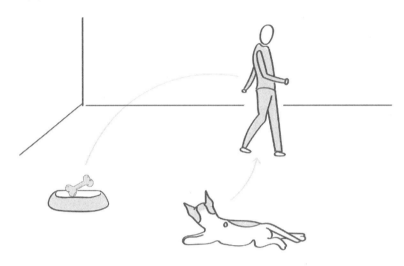

**Figure 12: Guarding from Distance**

Once you have claimed a power object using the Resource Guarding technique previously discussed, a very interesting phenomenon occurs that we can leverage in our training. After your dog fully surrenders (sits down, lies down, then places their chin on the floor), begin to slowly walk away from the power object.

As you walk away, make sure to angle your spine and your face so that you are looking at your dog the entire time. Your posture is key, because it does the following things all at once:

- It communicates to your dog that you don't fully trust them.
- It positions you in a place of power and says that you still own the resource.
- The fear generated from the use of the Forbidden Angle discourages your dog from attempting to steal the object.

The result of all of this is that your dog essentially lies still and pays attention to you. When you come back, you can reward it with the power object. It can take months to train a puppy a reliable "down-stay", but with this technique you achieve the same results in minutes.

# The Transformation

With Bon Jovi still lying down and breathing softly in front of "Sonia's" bowl of salmon at the top of the stairs, we systematically began the process of flooding his nervous system one common doorway-trigger at a time. While maintaining the Guarding the Line angle, I encouraged Sonia to approach the door, then walk back to Bon Jovi. He remained lying down, so we rewarded him with a piece of salmon. Then I asked her to introduce a variety of classic triggers that would stimulate anxiety for many dogs around doors. She jingled her keys, put her jacket on, took her jacket off, grabbed the leash (as if going for a walk), rang the doorbell, and even opened the door. After carrying out each of these potentially triggering activities, Sonia walked back to Bon Jovi and rewarded him with a piece of salmon for staying calmly in place.

Some triggers have the potential to activate a significant amount of stress in your dog, so you want to introduce them as softly as possible. If your dog gets too excited by the distraction, they will jump up and break their "down-stay." If this occurs, simply intensify your asset-guarding posture, or leverage the scent of the power object, to redirect your dog's energy. Always work with calmness.

During these exercises, I taught Sonia to pay special attention to Bon Jovi's posture and breathing pattern. We looked out for the subtlest clues denoting reactivity to each stimulus, because the goal was to keep him calm while he was being triggered.

Sonia was surprised at how easy it was for her to use gentle eye contact and a power object (barbecue salmon) to train this new behavior. Suddenly she danced around the foyer with the front door wide open, and her dog didn't even move an inch. Her posture began to transform as stress melted away. She appeared more confident and beautiful. Her spine grew, and her voice radiated a soft, loving tone. Sonia was becoming a completely different woman.

We decided to end the two-hour lesson by allowing Bon Jovi to eat the remaining salmon from the bowl, as a reward for demonstrating his newfound mental discipline. I told Sonia to give him a big rest for the remainder of the day in his meditation chamber (crate), sealing in the results from the intense energy work we had just performed. We agreed that I should come back again tomorrow to do another session, but I knew in my heart that Bon Jovi had already done all the hard work today. Once a dog learns what their Peaceful Alpha wants, they desire to give it to them all the time.

The next day when I rang the doorbell, I did not hear any barking. A few seconds later, Sonia opened the door with her eyes angled behind, communicating something assertive to Bon Jovi. She was "guarding the line," and he was lying down calmly at the top of the stairs. When she faced me, I noticed a big smile. This turned out to be the only lesson we needed to successfully curb Bon Jovi's escape problems for good.

Sonia called me a week later, after Thanksgiving, beaming with positive energy. She told me that she had put some turkey in Bon Jovi's bowl, placed it at the top of the stairs, and wouldn't let him touch it.  Each time a guest had arrived, she had rewarded his excellent behavior with a bit of the turkey. As the evening continued, he ignored the doorbell, remained calm, and savored his treats when they were given to him. For the rest of the night, Bon Jovi could be found lying on Sonia's foot under the table, like a perfect dog.

# Training Tips
## Lie Down and Stay

1. Place a high-value treat in your dog's bowl to create a power object you can use to control your dog's reactivity around other triggers.

2. Place the bowl on the ground, between your feet, using the asset-ownership position. Tap into the Forbidden Angle to communicate a minimal amount of fear, clarifying to your dog that this is your Power Object.

3. Harness the submissive response that is natural to your dog when an Alpha claims a resource. Wait for your dog to fully surrender into a lie-down, chin-down position. Name this behavior "Down," and reward your dog with a piece of the reward from the power object bowl.

4. Begin moving away from the resource, while "guarding the line." Be certain to assert yourself the moment your dog moves. They will lie back down naturally because their desire for the power object is their primary motivation.

5. As your dog gets comfortable with you walking away from the power object, name this behavior "Stay." Always come back and reward your dog while they are in a calm state.

6. Randomize the distance and direction you move away for optimal results. Intuitively, we might think it's better to build the distance in a linear fashion. This is not the case, because as you move farther and farther away, your dog catches on to the pattern. This makes them more likely to break the "stay" position, which is motivated by their desire to come find you or challenge you for the resource. It's much better to do a few

short distances, then a long one, then a medium one, followed by a short one, and so forth. Keep them on their toes.

7. Always set up your dog for success, and reward them with the power object you're "guarding." Finish on a positive note.

# Meditation

## The Pink Orb of Healing Protection

Sometimes it is beneficial to use our imagination to cultivate bravery because it helps us face the feeling of fear with peacefulness and confidence. Sit comfortably, or lie down on your back. Still your body, and bring your attention to the organic rhythm of your breath. Find it in one of three places: your belly, your chest, or the outer ridges of your nostrils. Remain unwaveringly focused on this place for several minutes, or as long as you want. With your imagination, start to surround your body with a pink egg-shape of light.

This color represents the all-loving, healing power of the Universe, and its energy is available to you anytime you call upon it. Slowly, start to allow the pink light to fill up the base of the egg. Let its warm, loving sensations envelope you from the bottom up. Imagine that your inner child is basking in the womb of the Universe. Feel their love. Know that this feeling is available to you anytime you need it.

# 8

# Mindful Leash Walking

When I pulled my rental car up to her driveway, Ella Mae and her pup were waiting excitedly for me outside. My client was a successful psychotherapist who lived alone with her white miniature poodle puppy Charlie Girl in a townhouse community in Boulder, Colorado.

People from all over the country sought Ella Mae's help to deal with their anxiety, stress, and depression disorders. Being a good communicator with people, however, rarely transfers to our dogs. With dogs, our words have little significance. To them, our bodies, actions, and emotions do all the talking. This is especially true while walking them.

I smiled, remembering yet again that our dogs are truly our reflections in so many ways. Ella Mae's sporty pink baseball hat and her turquoise Nike sneakers matched the color scheme of Charlie Girl's sweatshirt. Completing the ensemble was a fashionable leash bejeweled with fake diamond studs. Though the outfits were nice, Charlie Girl's behavior immediately caught my eye. The puppy was ignoring Ella Mae who had politely asked her to "please relax." Instead, the six-month-old spun circles around Ella's legs, tethering her with a six-foot lasso.

The dog's ferociously wagging tail and excited yipping created an embarrassing spectacle to say the least. Ella Mae's frustration only fueled her puppy's excitement even more. Unfortunately, these behaviors were only the tip of the iceberg. The young furry guru also lunged at skateboarders, chased leaves, and trembled in fear from the mysterious vibration of the garbage truck. Charlie's anxious emotions were the real culprits. Furthermore, Ella's leash handling techniques were unconsciously communicating all the wrong messages.

## Our Unconscious Walking Strategies

In my experience, if your dog walks poorly for you on the leash, your leadership personality likely falls into one of two unfortunate categories: from your dog's perspective (and perhaps others in your life), you are either a "pleaser" or a "controller."

If you are a pleaser, then you have a tendency to follow your dog wherever it desires to go. As a sensitive soul, you likely do this as an attempt to eliminate the persistent tension on your dog's neck. Perhaps you justify it with the belief that you are allowing your dog to enjoy the outdoors. There are two big costs here. The first is that you would find much more joy if your dog followed you like you follow them! The second is that your actions communicate your role as the follower in this relationship. Leadership is not something you can turn on or off with your dog. If you do not lead them outside, how can you expect them to listen to you inside the house?

For those who are "controllers," you tend to choke up on the leash at even the slightest threat of a looming uncertainty. Your intuition senses an upcoming lunge or tug from your dog, and the thought makes you nervous. While this technique prevents your dog from misbehaving, the problem is that this fear-based strategy is reactionary. Aside from temporarily suffocating your dog, shortening the leash when you feel anxious actually creates more tension—not to mention that it fails to consider your dog's feelings, the very reason they misbehave in the first place. Over the long run, the tension you're adding to the equation frustrates your dog;

they are simply anxious, afraid, or excited about what they sense. In these moments, they require your calm presence and guidance when giving the two essential walking commands.

# The "Stop" Command

"Stop" is one of the simplest commands you can teach your pet, but its versatility and efficacy will perhaps make it one of your favorite commands. From your dog's perspective, it means all of these things at the same time:

- Become still now, (standing, sitting, or lying down is fine).
- Eliminate all tension on the leash, and be calm.
- Focus your attention on me, and be receptive.
- Don't move until I release you.

This was the opening lesson I taught Ella Mae and Charlie Girl. Ella Mae preferred that I demonstrate it, rather than talk her through it. As such, I simply took the leash from Ella's hand, stepped to the side, and channeled some assertive eye contact to Charlie to quell her exuberance. This conflict-seeking action communicated that it was time to relax. Charlie responded with a high-pitched purr (to release her energy) and then looked away from me and yawned (two Calming Signals). The tension she was creating in the leash instantly went slack, but the work was only just beginning. At this moment, I named the behavior I was trying to shape by saying "Stop."

The secret of this command is to trick your dog into thinking that you are a solid wooden post, because a post never follows the dog. Figure 13, on page 98, will help solidify the training exercise for this enlightened command. Charlie tugged me, accustomed to uprooting her mom at will. As I held steady, she took to exploring every direction that the radius of the leash allowed her to go. I remained aloof to her efforts, because I have done this enough to know how the story ends. Her excitement was quickly turning into anxiety. At this stage, it is normal for your pet to attempt to release the stress of not knowing what you want it to do by scratching its neck, whining, chewing its feet, or trying to put something in its mouth. All of this is fine, normal actually. This is possibly the first time your dog is not getting what it wants while on the leash.

All dogs will eventually come to realize that they are the ones creating the tension. Be silent, and do not add any extra energy to the equation. What we want to teach them, then reinforce, is that they have the power to eliminate this stress themselves.

Several minutes later, Charlie started yawning and looking at me with a raised paw. I explained to Ella that these two Calming Signals suggested that we were getting close. Within seconds, Charlie sat down, then lay down and put her chin on the ground, completing the predictable Sequence of Surrender. "Good Girl," I said softly. Then I threw a chunk of liver treat between her paws. I wanted to encourage her to remain in the lying-down position. Aha, her eyes twinkled, my new master wants me to do this when he says "Stop."

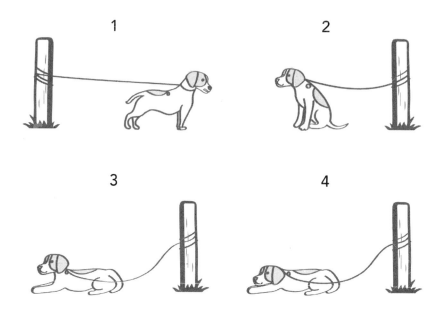

**Figure 13: Dog Tied to Post**

Let's take a look at what goes on inside a dog's mind-body when they are tied to a post.

**Step 1:** At first, the dog begins exploring. They pull this way and that, much like a typical dog would on a walk with their owner. Quickly, the dog discovers that they cannot move the post. Their emotions kick in. They feel frustrated, yet the more they pull, the more they come to realize that they are the ones who are creating the tension in the leash. This is but another example as to why dogs are furry gurus.

**Step 2:** Once they understand that they are the ones creating tension, they seek to eliminate it for themselves. At first, they sit and wait. This posture is a little too uncomfortable for a dog to hold for longer than a few minutes, so they surrender into something more pleasant.

**Step 3:** Once they are lying down, the surface area of their bellies make solid contact with the earth. It's almost like a grounding effect begins to take place.

**Step 4:** You can sense the moment when they fully surrender into peace and ease because it's always accompanied with a big sigh and the placement of their chins on the earth.

A good leash handler understands this process and leverages the predictable outcome while they train their dog. I'm proposing that you leash your dog, stand like a post (early in the walk, and often throughout it), and as you say the "Stop" command. Praise your dog when it reaches steps 2 through 4. Release your dog from this command by saying "Let's go," then continue walking.

# "Let's Go"

If you have ever seen a mama duck swimming while her babies calmly follow in her wake, then nature has shown you what a harmonious "Let's Go" command ought to look like.

The first step in teaching this to your dog is to forget everything you know about going for a walk. We are no longer interested in traveling from A to B efficiently. The second step is to begin meandering aimlessly with your pet. The strategic intention is to keep your body ahead of your dog at all times. Every now and then say "Stop," and become a post until your dog finds stillness. Then repeat the sequence. Say "Let's Go," and wander in circular patterns, keeping the leash as loose as possible.

I recommend practicing this for the first time in an open field, empty parking lot, or quiet street to minimize distractions and maximize success—even better, find an isolated place in the forest. The resonance of nature will clear your mind and elevate your consciousness.

If your dog moves out from behind you, a cue that it is distracted or attempting to take the lead, you have all kinds of options. The important thing is that you must react efficiently, discouraging it from taking on the role of leader. For example, if your dog zags left, then simply zig right and keep walking. The key is to pick a new direction, so that your dog's relative location is no longer in front of you but back behind you. Do this exercise continuously for up to 15 minutes. Eventually, your dog will discover that it can never lead you! It will communicate this act of surrender by dropping its head, following you, and matching your pace perfectly.

# Rules for Walking Past Other Dogs

The art of mindful walking enriches the calm connection between you and your pet at all times. When a Peaceful Alpha sees another dog out on a walk, we do not view it as either an opportunity for a "play date" or socialization. That is what puppy play dates or visits to the dog park are for; otherwise, the attention your dog pays to other dogs will always create tension in the leash. Just playing a few times with other dogs encountered on walks unfortunately teaches your dog to walk in front of you and tug toward every animal it sees, so in this regard, transmuting tension in the leash needs to be a rather businesslike affair.

The polite thing to do when walking your dog past another dog is to communicate that you have non-playful yet peaceful intentions. You want both your dog and the dog you're passing to know that you're not interested in aggression nor in playing. Communicate this to all parties by placing your dog on the other side of any dogs you encounter and walking past the dogs in an arc. Gauge the size of the arc needed by the reactivity of the dogs in question. If both dogs remain calm and tension-free on the leash, then of course a polite bum sniff is acceptable. Just don't linger; get on with the walk. It is easier to keep a calm dog calm than it is to calm it down after it has become excited.

## Rules for Walking Past Other People

Sometimes when we are mindfully walking our dog, we encounter someone who wants to greet our dog. You know that stopping to meet this person will be disruptive to your flow, yet the "teddy bear" effect of your dog lures that person toward you anyway. They simply want to soak up your dog's love, and who can blame them?

As a Peaceful Alpha, your best option is to sensitively avoid this situation until you have conditioned your dog to be calm in all surroundings. It's polite to give a quiet nod, or a subtle wave from a distance to these people. This acknowledges that we see them, but when they see us arcing around them using the protective posture, they understand that we're "training" our dogs, and they don't take it personally.

# The Transformation

Three months later I returned to Colorado. I called Ella Mae to check in, and we made plans to go for another walk that Sunday at 7 a.m. When I pulled into her street, I saw a completely different picture from the previous one. Ella was sitting on a wooden bench near her garden. The scent coming off the native flowering serviceberry bush was intoxicatingly pleasant. Her outfit was much different than before. The modest poncho rested over her head as she meditated. Charlie was sporting a thin brown leather leash, making it much more practical for mindful walking. One end was connected to Charlie, who lay resting with her belly on the damp grass.

Ella thanked me for coming early. Charlie followed suit, offering me a silent tail wag and a couple of intentional blinks. This calm acknowledgment was her way of mimicking her mistress's communication to me. Oh yes, our dogs certainly are our reflections. Ella pointed out that her young furry guru currently was settled in the "Stop" command. Their new walking routine began with a quick pee to relieve her pup's bladder, followed by a 15-minute meditation in the garden.

"Let's go," Ella whispered. Charlie calmly stood, and the morning walk began with a few warm-up drills. Ella meandered slowly and deliberately around her garden. Charlie, already in the flow state from the meditation, proudly followed in her mom's wake. Ella transitioned into some "Stop" and "Go" work, walking up and down the stone driveway.

"Are you ready, Jesse?" Ella asked me with a mischievous grin. "Then, let's go." She winked at me and the three of us enjoyed a wonderfully relaxed and refreshing 20-minute walk through the neighborhood. Ella steered Charlie, confidently arcing around other dogs and various distractions. I was astounded with the transformation in both dog and owner. Charlie followed her mom on a loose leash that never made contact with the ground, while Ella was becoming a true Peaceful Alpha.

# Training Tips
## Leash Walking

1. Your dog takes directional cues about where you are leading it by watching where your eyes are pointing.

2. Looking at your dog while it is leashed unconsciously miscommunicates that you think it is the leader. It will want to pull you.

3. Dogs must first learn to absorb their surroundings in calmness and stillness before they learn to walk in these surroundings among distractions.

4. We should be mindful of where we position our hand on the leash, and how much slack we allow.

5. Whether stopping or going, the leash must be in the shape of a "hook."

6. Don't hold the leash in the same spot for the entire walk. Be fluid with your hand position to help facilitate the shape of the "hook." This helps your dog have more space to remain calm.

# Meditation

## Standing like a Golden Post

Take your dog to a quiet park. Trees are sentient beings; they are alive and conscious of you. Find one that feels good to you, and stand underneath it with your feet together. Hook a thumb through the handle of the leash, and interlace your hands. Rest them on your lower belly. This is your energetic power source. Learning how to feel this and fill it up with your mind is an ancient trick that helps us remain calm and conscious throughout our daily life.

Physical stillness is important. It leads to stillness in our minds. Effortlessness is equally important, because it allows us to use our energy to access deeper states of meditation. While standing, our body learns to relax when our inner legs are firmly connected to one another. Our anatomy knows to hold us up effortlessly. We don't need to think about it, only feel it.

Remain still, and take a few conscious, slow inhalations and exhalations. Do a scan of your body with your mind. Feel your entire body. Feel your toes, feet, shins, knees, legs, and pelvis. Feel your trunk, shoulders, arms, and neck. Feel your head resting softly on the top of your spine. Feel the crown of your head.

Your feet are the base of your "tree." Imagine that you have invisible roots extending from them that drop deeply into the earth. Visualize your roots interweaving with the dirt and the roots of the actual tree you're standing under.

Start to stretch your inhalations and exhalations to a smooth count of four. As you inhale, imagine that you're drawing in golden light from the leaves of the trees through the crown of your head. As you exhale, allow this golden nectar to drip down your body into your belly, your power source.

On your next inhale, imagine that you're purifying your energetic center of any toxins. Exhale, and visualize a release of black energy. Watch it flush down your legs, through the roots of your feet. Let the earth receive it, and recycle it. She's the mother of all living beings; she'll always help us purify our energy if we're open to her.

Repeat this cycle of breathing and visualization for 10 minutes, or as long as you want. When you're ready to leave, take a few mindful breaths, and notice what your dog is up to. What position are they in? What does harmony look like at this moment? Then with your softest voice, say

"Let's go," and flow together like the gentle wind.

# 9

# Zen and the Art of Deflating Aggression

One evening I received an emergency call from Malachi. His voice had the authority you might expect from a 48-year-old CEO. It also carried the tone of a man feeling great sadness. At his San Francisco–based start-up in California, every day was bring-your-dog-to-work day; they even had a company dog walker.

The dog walker had just informed Malachi that his dog Donna was now kicked out of their lunchtime pack. The walker had grown tired of the way the 80-pound Doberman instigated fights.

Stories of Donna's aggression were beginning to swirl around the office as well. A few days ago, Gail from the sales department extended the back of her hand toward Donna, attempting to make a friendly connection. The Straight Line Encounter (SLE) of this well-intended gesture spooked the dog into making an air snap. Though her teeth did not break any skin, Gail's shirt was not so lucky. Donna's teeth caught the fabric and shredded it from the elbow down. Gail surely didn't intend to generate fear in Donna, but please take a look at Figure 14 at the end of this section to understand what the communication of her reaching out to Donna felt like to the dog.

Malachi wanted to nip this embarrassing situation in the bud. How could he maintain his credibility as CEO when his dog stirred things up daily at the office? He knew that the only way his aggressive furry guru would be welcome back in the office was if she underwent a massive transformation. I could tell from his tone how much he loved Donna.

"She has such a tender and loving side that only I know about. Can you help us?"

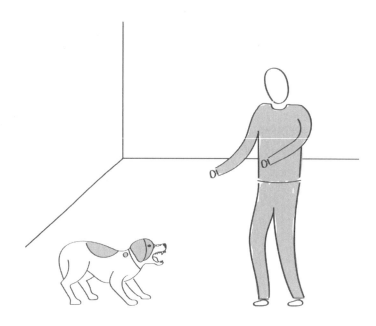

**Figure 14: Dog in a Corner**

There's an old adage, which is completely false by the way. It suggests that you should reach out the back of your hand to greet a new dog. While the intention of this gesture has love and friendliness at heart, according to the Secret Language of Dogs, it is entirely misguided. In this illustration, the dog has already placed themselves in the corner.

Their action suggests an attempt to make themselves feel safe (nothing can sneak up behind you from this vantage). It's a cue that they are perhaps lacking confidence. We can also see that the dog's tail is curled up underneath their legs and their ears are pointed, both signs of caution.

The big tell, however, is that as the human approaches, looks at the dog, and reaches out their hand to offer a sniff, a significant violation of the Forbidden Angle has just occurred. No wonder Donna snapped at Gail. It was a communication. The frightened dog was only trying to use offense to make her feel safe.

# Through the Eyes of an Aggressive Dog

The office reception area was spacious and lacked a secretary. I looked down the hallway and noticed that Malachi's office was located in the corner. For the moment, his opaque door remained shut. I could see Donna's enormous silhouette hovering on the inside, guarding their territory. She probably heard me get off the elevator, then mobilized herself into this protective position, tipping Malachi off to my arrival. Suddenly, he flung the door open with too much muscle, creating a jarring noise that exacerbated his dog's fear.

"Hey, Jesse. Come on in!" Malachi greeted me with a charming South African accent. His handshake was as aggressive as his door slam. "You gotta meet Donna; she is the sweetest," he said enthusiastically.

I was reluctant to oblige. It did not seem to me that he was tuned into his dog's emotions at all. Donna had now positioned herself directly in front of her master, fully assuming the protective posture. When I glanced at her, she raised her lip and showed me her fangs, not the friendliest gesture. The hair on the nape of her neck was standing tall, and her tail quivered between her hind legs. I exhaled and noticed that Donna's spiked collar and muscular chest accentuated the intimidating presence that she was bred for. Then I heard her make an almost undetectable growl, and it gave me the chills.

I wanted to set the dog at ease, so I took an exaggerated step backward and yawned in her direction. I encouraged Malachi to stand closer to me, assuming the guarding position himself, then to stare at his dog for a few seconds. The lesson had already begun. Luckily, our combined actions communicated that I could be trusted. Eventually, the frightened furry guru took her focused eyes off me and slowly retreated under Malachi's desk, where she continued to watch me cautiously.

# Understanding Aggression

We seldom give consideration to the intentions behind an aggressive act; the truth is, scaring others is an easy way to manipulate them. But if dogs are inherently peaceful, why would they want to do that? Most of the time, it is because your dog is hurting from a physical pain or emotional wound.

Consider a puppy with a sprained knee. Were you to try to dog it, it might very well attempt to bite you to prevent you from hurting it more. Another example would be a dog that is remembering pain from a past experience, such as a dog that bites when you try to clip their nails. They are not in pain now, but they are remembering a time when the groomer took the nails too short, misjudging where the nerve endings lie.

In both cases, these acts of aggression are really just indicators of how the dog is feeling right now. Proceeding mindlessly just pours gas on the fire. Dogs have an emotional memory, and this is what we leverage when we train them like a Peaceful Alpha.

The easiest way to deflate aggression in any being is to make them feel safe. The safer you make them feel, the more quickly they will relax. The first step in doing this is to heighten your level of attunement. As a Peaceful Alpha, you have to stay connected to your energy, the environment, and your dog's feelings as often as possible. Acting with swiftness is the key to dealing with aggression, because the energy of aggression accumulates momentum really quickly. There are many ways up the mountain. The beautiful thing about the Secret Language of Dogs is that there are always multiple solutions to the same problem.

# Commanding With Respect and Love

The protective posture, also known as the body-guarding stance, is the Peaceful Alpha's way of communicating safety to their dog. Malachi could command Donna to get behind him while he attuned himself to her body language; showering her with his own Calming Signals, such as yawning or blinking at her, would help her feel safe and able to calm down. In addition to this, a Kung Fu Finger on the nape of her neck would serve as insurance. Were she to react, he would be literally on top of her, controlling the situation.

A master's duty never turns off, because their dog's emotions never turn off. When you remain alert, calm, and in command, this allows your dog to find serenity, knowing that you have got the territory covered.

## Power Objects

Malachi could redirect Donna's attention to a power object, and place it under his desk (where she likes to lie down). It might be a stuffed KONG, rawhide, or another high-value chew treat, which essentially acts as a distraction from any fear she might be experiencing. Redirecting Donna's attention to the activity of chewing would allow her to release her energy productively.

When we understand the magnetic force of power objects on our dog's minds and emotions, it just seems wise to keep a variety of them on hand. Your pup will love the spontaneous "activity time" you provide it with, and they will not think twice about the fact that you are redirecting them away from doing something bad.

## Enlightened Crate Training

In our lesson, I recommended that Malachi provide Donna with a crate in the back corner of his office. Donna is a scary-looking dog, and workers who were not comfortable with her appearance often complained of feeling afraid. That fear would trigger Donna's aggression each time.

The solution of crate training mitigates that risk entirely. When employees came to his office, he could simply command Donna to go to her sanctuary and meditate. She would feel protected and safe there, especially if it were covered with a blanket. If the sanctuary looked discreet, visitors could then be oblivious to her presence. Remember, crates feel a lot like dens to dogs. These little habitats have a natural, calming effect on them. Providing our pup with a safe place they can go dramatically reduces aggression, simply because it makes the dog so much calmer.

## Know Thy Dog

As we begin the journey of attuning ourselves to our dog, it is imperative that we study each aggressive situation from a place of peace and nonreactivity. Consider the reasons why a dog might attack: territorial; protective instinct; possessiveness (over a resource, toy, person, and so on); lack of social experience; frustration; physical pain; fear; defensiveness; or hormonal (unneutered, sexual, mating).

Depending on the severity of the aggression, and due to safety concerns, it often makes sense to work with a professional trainer. Just a single outburst of aggression is a liability that exacerbates our own stress level, something our dog will surely be able to feel.

## The Transformation

A month later I made my return visit to Malachi's workplace. As soon as I stepped off the elevator, Malachi was waiting for me, standing well in front of his office door, looking like a true Peaceful Alpha. He was calm, quiet, confident, and embodying the protective posture. I wondered where Donna was. Malachi's voice was incredibly soft and warm, and he invited me into his office.

As I was walking toward it, strangely enough, I noticed that there was no more slobber along the bottom window. Malachi beamed with pride, as he reflected on how Donna used to huff and puff on the glass every time her territorial instincts flared. I was impressed by his increased level of attunement.

Finally I spotted Donna, lying down with her chin on the floor. She was on her mat, which was in the far corner of the office. On the floor, in front of her nose, was a smoked elk antler, an irresistible organic chew treat. Donna's eyes were soft and entirely focused on her master. Wherever Malachi went, her eyes followed. She was disciplined, and she was waiting for the command signaling that she was allowed to chew this "resource."

She remained that way while I sat down and listened to Malachi's update. This version of Donna didn't look frightening to me in the least. Her relaxed muscles, glistening black coat, and calm presence made her look majestic. I asked if I could go and pet her, and Malachi peacefully, yet assertively, told me it wasn't a good idea because he did not want to break her command. He said that the company dog walker would be up momentarily to take her out with the pack, based on her improved behavior, and that would be an ideal moment for me to pet her.

Malachi shared some of the personal transformation he had experienced in this last month too. He noticed that he had not been as attuned to his employees as he could have been. In fact, he was rather abrupt with them, with incredible expectations that didn't really seem fair. Once he learned how to listen to Donna's feelings, he also experienced a softening in his attitude toward his team.

He reflected that they were scared of saying no to any of his requests. He used to get angry and disappointed when they did not deliver according to his expectations. He now realized that they were simply saying yes to him because they were scared. Through his work with Donna, Malachi's emotional intelligence blossomed. He suddenly cared about his workers' feelings and sought to improve their working conditions by improving his communication. He soon discovered that the more he stayed unconditionally present with his employees, the better he became at communicating the company's objectives to them. Productivity and office morale became much higher, while Donna's stress level became much lower – everyone became more relaxed in this environment.

# Training Tips
## Using a Clicker to Stop Aggression

The following method is an incredibly popular approach to quickly and humanely teach dogs how to find comfort in many situations that would otherwise trigger their aggression. This method can be replicated in many different scenarios.

### Phase 1 – Introducing the Clicker to Your Dog

1. First, we teach your dog to associate the sound of the clicker with the pleasure of receiving a high-value treat. Out of sight of your dog, set aside about two dozen bite-sized rewards.

2. When your dog is not suspecting it, use the clicker to make a noise and then give it a reward. Work in silence, and repeat this whenever your dog stops paying attention to you. Rather quickly, the click will form a positive association. Your dog will begin looking at you, focusing on you, and anticipating a treat.

### Phase 2 – Using the Clicker to Signal, Rewire, and Reward

3. Begin with your dog leashed and far enough away from the trigger (such as a stranger) that it doesn't feel threatened. The whole point is to avoid flaring up their defensive tendencies, such as growling, lunging, snapping, or biting.

4. When your dog is calm, use the clicker to make a clicking noise and then reward your dog.

5. Gradually approach the trigger in an arc. After a few steps, stop, click, and reward.

6. Take another step closer, click, and reward. We are rewiring your dog's fearful response to one of trust and pleasure. Continue this sequence, at a safe distance, and remain patient. Use your protective bodyguard angle and soft tone of voice to generate the feeling of safety and reassure your dog.

7. Gradually move closer to the trigger, and continue clicking and praising.

8. Your dog will begin to learn that the trigger equals a treat, and it will naturally shift its focus onto you.

# Meditation

### Attuning Yourself to Yourself

Close your eyes, and sit comfortably in front of a mirror, either cross-legged on the floor or upright in a chair. Be still, and find your connection to the ground. Feel your seat bones sink into the firm surface. Let this connection with the earth become the foundation of your awareness. Let your imagination begin to spread from the base of your spine, into your hips, down your thigh bones, past your knees and ankles, and into your toes. Let the earth receive your roots, and allow her to counter the effects of gravity on your spine. Breathe into your backbone, and settle into a tall but comfortable position so that your crown can open to the sky.

Bring your awareness into your belly, chest, upper throat, and nasal cavity. Don't try to modify it or spread it to a new location. Practice attuning yourself to the inner workings of your breath while you restrain yourself from trying to make it something else. This is the practice of giving space. Trust that an organic intelligence, which is greater than our intellect, will take over and send your life force to where it needs to go.

When you feel centered and peaceful, open your eyes and look into the mirror. How long can you make eye contact with yourself before you instinctively turn away? It's you that you're looking at. There's no need to avoid the reflection, yet we tend to do this instinctively.

Close your eyes, center yourself again, then come back to the eye contact you see in the mirror. This time, take 10 conscious breaths while you maintain eye contact with yourself. Attune to yourself. What new sensations are arriving? Where is your body contorting? What does your face look like? What emotions are beginning to flow? Observe these things without judgment, and let them all go.

# 10

# Abundant Happiness and Vitality for You and Your Dog

Discovering true mental health is a journey we all face in our lives. Luckily, we have three kinds of wisdom teachers who help guide us along the way. These teachers always arrive in the same order, and they never appear until the student is ready. First comes Pain, which points us toward Silence, which nudges us toward Love, which in turn teaches us how to find that sweet nectar of abundance that is our birthright.

Our dogs, furry gurus as they are, have much to teach us about compassion and joy. We needn't look farther than the principles of the Secret Language of Dogs to see that each non-conflict-seeking action a dog takes is rooted in presence and kindness. The essence of Calming Signals communicates peace, harmony, and safety. Love is on a dog's mind 24/7.

In our materialistic culture, mainstream society often puts profit ahead of love. The result of this programming is that our unconscious minds internalize false beliefs about how we ought to live our lives. We are taught that buying things makes us happy; yet, once we acquire any of our desires, our happiness is fleeting.

On the journey of becoming a Peaceful Alpha, we commit to continuously entering the stream of the present moment so that we can connect with our dog and communicate with them in real time.

As this process unfolds, you will naturally overcome all kinds of bad habits or distractions you once relied on to soothe your intense feelings.

These habits once served us well. They helped us soothe anxieties or chronic pain we could not understand. Escapism impedes our ability to connect to the present moment, causing us to miss all kinds of opportunities to communicate with our dog. It also keeps us in a state of low consciousness, which in a roundabout way, births all kinds of undesirable behaviors in your furry guru.

The journey of becoming a Peaceful Alpha, and the real-life teachings you receive from your furry guru, shine a light on all of our unconscious behaviors and programming. Slowly, layers of conditioning will start peeling back in your psyche. Wisdom and compassion arrive of their own accord, and the grip of the ego relaxes. The Law of Attraction, which we will soon learn about, continues to do its thing. You become happier, healthier, wealthier and wiser. This process happens naturally; you don't even have to think about it.

## What True Mental Health Feels Like

Imagine it is cold outside and you and your dog just returned from a Sunday walk through the forest. Inside your home, a crackling fire warms up the den. You feel like taking a rest, so you nestle into your favorite reading chair in front of the fireplace. You look down on the rug and notice a cute collection of your dog's favorite treasures—old chew sticks, a squeaky rubber chicken, a used tennis ball, and one of your gym socks—which start to fill you with joy.

You hone your Peaceful Alpha focus by savoring this sensation for around 20 seconds, long enough for the law of attraction to create a momentum of happiness for the rest of the day. This focusing technique short-cuts you into abundance and well-being, and we will revisit it later in the chapter.

Soon you and your dog drift off into a pleasant Sunday afternoon snooze. As you're falling asleep, your consciousness shifts out of the talking mind into pure awareness, the optimal state of mental health. There are no thoughts right now. Your muscles are at ease, and your breathing is rhythmic. Your body feels comfortable, and your mind and emotions are tranquil. The concept of optimal mental health is rarely discussed, yet in the moments before we drift off to sleep, we can experience its perfection ever so briefly.

As you learn to maintain this presence for longer periods, through your meditation and Peaceful Alpha work, you will discover that this feeling of well-being starts snowballing. You won't have to work as hard to find it; it just arrives naturally. This powerful phenomenon is quite useful for a Peaceful Alpha. It heightens your presence and attunes you much more deeply to your dog, allowing you to be in a position to always command with respect and love. This was certainly the case for my student, Anthony, who you will soon meet.

## Heal Ourselves, Heal Our Dogs

Our minds and bodies are inseparable. When we pollute our bodies with sugar, cigarettes, alcohol, or any poor choice for that matter, we can't help but feel the effects in our minds. Poison in the body affects our focus, clarity, and emotions. It leads to lethargy and empowers the unconscious cycle of negative thinking. Similarly, when the quality of our thoughts is negative, judgmental, or toxic in any way, it generates unpleasant emotions that present themselves in the body. Our mind affects our body, and our body affects our mind. As a Peaceful Alpha, we must pay attention to everything we ingest (food, beverages, medicines, and so on), observe our underlying motivation, and how it makes us feel later.

"The apple never falls far from the tree," as the saying goes, also applies to our dogs: the state of our physical and mental health affects their well-being. This happens whether we're thinking about it or not, as was the case with my client Anthony. Chewy, his three-year-old yellow lab, suffered from obesity, chronic stomach problems, loss of hair, itchy skin, and weak hips. Instead of pooping once or twice a day, excreting a perfectly torpedo-shaped plop, Chewy would sometimes go three times per walk and squirt out something that resembled the consistency of soft-serve ice cream.

As a result, Chewy was a very whiny and anxious dog.

Anthony himself was overweight, ate fast food multiple times a week, never exercised, and had a nervous stomach from poor diet and chronic anxiety. He had never considered that digestion could be used as a barometer for health, not until pain showed up and motivated him to make a serious change.

One day, Anthony spontaneously had a panic attack while he was driving the local transit bus along a busy street. He watched himself temporarily lose control of the vehicle. The intense fright of the experience immediately cleared his consciousness. It sobered him to the fact that he'd been making very poor choices for himself. Per my recommendation, Anthony started meditating every morning before he walked his dog. I casually suggested the role that food plays on our emotions, both ours and our dog's, and it really resonated with Anthony.

He became inspired to begin eating consciously. His intention was to nourish his body as optimally as possible. Simply by tuning in to how he felt after eating, and by doing some basic research online, Anthony started tinkering with his diet. He started paying attention to the clarity he'd notice when he ate clean foods. He discovered that meat-heavy meals made him feel sluggish for hours after eating, and that fasting helped him clean out his organs and revitalize his energy levels. He also noticed that eating unprocessed, nutrient-dense, plant-based superfoods left him the most energized, clear-headed, with a zest for life. Pain and Silence had inspired Anthony to begin making Loving choices.

Noticing the profound health benefits in his life, Anthony stopped feeding Chewy low-quality processed snacks. He also realized that purchasing low-cost, non-perishable, value-sized bags of kibble were money-saving decisions and were not motivated from the heart. Soon, he cut out all the guilty treats.

Per my recommendation, he started feeding Chewy raw meat, bones, and organs, because these are superfoods for dogs. In only one month, Chewy's digestion issues completely vanished, the hair on his coat grew back, his itching stopped, and his digestion became impeccable. Dogs are smart. They know who's feeding them, and they know how the food makes them feel. When they see their life improve as a result of the choices we make on their behalf, their love and respect for us only grows, as does your Peaceful Alpha power.

## Harnessing the Law of Attraction

The Law of Attraction, much like the concept of Calming Signals, is always occurring. What we think and feel sends a vibration into the Universe. This happens whether we are aware of it or not. The Universe senses our emotions and mysteriously sends us events, people, and ideas that will generate more of the same feelings we are presently experiencing. When we are stuck in our heads, ruminating about the past or the future, we attract people, things, and experiences that make us feel worried or anxious.

Alternatively, when we are happy, vital, and excited about life, the Universe delivers in kind. Once we can shift the momentum of our feelings by seizing control of our mental and physical health, all areas of our life begin to improve naturally.

Deciding to improve your well-being is precisely how you leverage the Law of Attraction.

Let us revisit what happens with Anthony and Chewy to see how the Universe takes care of the rest, on his behalf.

Through his daily practice of meditation and a commitment to make loving choices for himself, Anthony became increasingly conscious of his thoughts and feelings. He saw the positive impact his diet was making on his mind-body. He continued looking for more opportunities to rev up his energy and cultivate a positive attitude so that he could feel even better. Anthony noticed that daily exercise helped in all of these areas, especially if he did it first thing in the morning. He began taking Chewy on 30-minute power marches on quiet forest trails. He'd leave his own power objects (his phone and his music) in the car and focus on the sounds of nature as he worked out.

As he exercised mindfully, he experienced even more positive effects on his mental health. This is when the transformational results in both Anthony and Chewy started to become exponential. Releasing endorphins first thing in the morning left Anthony feeling focused and pleasant all day long, allowing him to be incredibly in tune and patient with Chewy (two virtues of a true Peaceful Alpha). Aside from making him a better master for his dog, it also increased his metabolism, invigorated him, and accelerated his weight loss.

Chewy benefited tremendously from this new regime of mindful morning exercise as well. He shed layers of fat and developed lean muscles. The mobility of his hind legs improved, rebalancing and healing his hip condition. In order to keep up with his fast-marching master, Chewy naturally stopped focusing on all the glorious smells of the forest and the temptation of the squirrels. The happy lab surrendered to the rhythmic pace that Anthony, his Peaceful Alpha, established. The two were walking in harmony, without a leash. Anthony was not sure how he trained his dog to do this, but he chalked it up to their increased connection with one another. The other reason is that Anthony was behaving like a powerful Peaceful Alpha. When a leader marches with purpose, their dog instinctively knows to follow.

Through the Law of Attraction, the Universe began delivering abundance into all pillars of Anthony's life. Now his pleasant disposition and passion for his colleagues and clients earned him an unexpected promotion at work. Losing weight, along with an increased level of vitality, made Anthony look and feel more attractive. His confidence was at an all-time high. Within a few months, the Law of Attraction did its thing again. Without any expectations, Anthony had suddenly received a promotion at work and attracted a beautiful romance into his life after several years of being single.

As health and wellness continued to abound in Anthony's life, the feeling of gratitude and trust in the Universe naturally started replacing the old patterns of anxiety and worry. Anthony's deep presence and clarity allowed him to blossom into a thriving Peaceful Alpha. Chewy loved his master's new energy, and over time transformed into a stoic, well-tempered dog—the kind that requires no training and just seems to behave calmly (almost) all of the time. This sort of transformational work is not only about fixing your dog's behaviors; it's about improving yourself, developing your wisdom, and living in harmony with the Universe. Just like it did for Anthony, when you walk the path of the Peaceful Alpha, the Law of Attraction delivers wonderful blessings into your life.

# Training Tips
## The Well-Being of Your Dog

1. Feed yourself and your dog loving foods.

2. A raw meat diet is optimal for a dog's health. It keeps their teeth white and their coats radiant. It also reduces lipomas, which can be caused from the typical preservatives found in kibble. You can now buy this at most pet shops, or you can make your own.

3. The way we feel and behave affects how our dog feels and behaves.

4. We can make ourselves feel better by savoring pleasant emotions. Focusing on this for as little as 20 seconds shifts the momentum of your mood.

5. In the mornings, before you meditate, try making lists of things that make you feel good. Savor the feelings as long as possible. Your meditation experience will be profound.

6. The Law of Attraction is never not working. Maximize its effects on purpose. Elevate your vibration by spending time with your joyful dog. Leave your phone at home, and get out into nature with your dog. This will amplify your vibration, allowing you to leverage the Law of Attraction.

When you feel clear, confident, healthy, and powerful, commanding with respect and love becomes natural. A dog desires this from its master and will behave calmly and stoically for you. This is the natural relationship between human and dog, and you're close to achieving it.

# Meditation

## Generating Manifestations

Rest in a comfortable position—either flat on your back, sitting cross-legged on the floor, or lying on a bed. Choose a quiet environment with no distractions. Allow your body to settle into a conscious stillness. Bring your attention to your organic breathing pattern, and simply observe it. Label the cycle of your breath mentally: silently say "Hello" on the inhale; "Hello" in the space between the inhale and exhale; and "Hello" on the exhale. Continue this cycle for several minutes until your energy shifts. Bringing a friendly, inner commentary to a simple labeling exercise will lighten your mood, because this thought is an action that generates a loving frequency.

Once your mind has become stabilized, continue to use the power of imagination to raise your vibration and change your emotion into something pleasant.

Visualize yourself resting in front of a beautiful fireplace. Hear the crackle of the fire. Feel its warmth on your skin. Smell the smoke.

Begin imagining all the people you love dearly. One by one, visualize them standing behind you. See yourself resting in front of the fire and your loved ones in the same scene. Pay attention to the people who make you feel warm and fuzzy and bask in the emotion that's being generated by the thought of each person. No need to rush through the list of people. In fact, the entire exercise is meant to generate momentum of positive feeling emotions. That's it. Do your best to sustain the pleasant feeling, and continuously pivot your thoughts into more positive-feeling directions.

After you've cycled through the imagery of the fire and visualized all the people you love standing behind you, it's time to simply breathe again and stop thinking. Just breathe organically, and enjoy the pleasantness of the emotion you've cultivated. Our thoughts and emotions are simply vibrations. The Law of Attraction states that "Like vibration attracts like vibration." That means that experiences and material objects you desire, ones that will make you feel good, will soon begin arriving.

Using meditation, thought, and your feeling intelligence, you're changing your energy. You're becoming an energetic magnet of positive attraction. The secret now is to become incredibly clear on the things you want in your life. For once you know your desires, and once you maintain an elevated vibration, the magical element of life begins to enliven. Get ready; you're about to receive everything you have ever wanted: health, love, wealth, and the most valuable treasure of them all, inner peace.

# 11

# Adoption
## Earning Trust and Opening Hearts

Nikki and Rikki met at Pride Week on Rhode Island seven years ago. It was the magnetic energy of their three-year-old bulldogs that drew the shy couple together. Nikki, a retired professional athlete, managed several fitness clubs on the East Coast. Rikki, a Pilates teacher and life coach, taught at a variety of studios nearby. Coincidentally, one woman owned an English bulldog named Thelma and the other an American bulldog named Louise.

Over the years, Thelma and Louise played, cuddled, and slobbered all over one another. They benevolently shared the resources (their parents) and territory (the king-size bed) with a precious love. All that raw food, glucosamine, reiki, and CBD oil had allowed the bulldogs to age gracefully beyond their years, but they were fast approaching the end of their road.

As Nikki and Rikki contemplated their future, they couldn't imagine life without a dog. The couple decided that they wanted to adopt a young whippersnapper. Perhaps, they intuited, a puppy's zest would inject some new energy into the bulldogs.

## Wisdom, Restraint, and the Law of Attraction

There are several considerations dog owners should reflect upon before they acquire a new companion. For instance, what type of lifestyle do you enjoy (active or relaxed)? Have you researched a variety of breeds and their characteristics? Can you afford the additional costs such as food, veterinary care, and pet shop expenditures? What will their grooming requirements be in terms of frequency and effort? And finally, do you have the desire to train, exercise, and integrate a new dog into your household?

Nikki, Rikki, and I covered these topics during a recent conference call. However, what they shared with me next gave me chills. They wanted to tap into the power of the Law of Attraction and let the Universe deliver the perfect dog to them.

# The Perfect Dog Awaits

Nikki and Rikki placed ads on several local classified websites and waited patiently. Eventually, if the perfect dog was out there, they knew they would be guided to it through their intuitions. The couple desired a small canine that would adapt to their lifestyle over the next decade. In order to help attract a good match, they imagined traveling with it, sneaking it into their hotels, even taking it to their fitness clubs. Nikki went so far as to envision carrying their future little furry guru in one of those fashionable backpacks that doubles as a functional crate in disguise. It's worth noting, all of these visualizations made them feel wonderful, which only accelerated the manifestation process.

Through practicing meditation over the years, Nikki and Rikki had developed incredible power over their own focus. They were using it, along with their imaginations, to communicate with the Universe on purpose. Remember, your present-moment thoughts and feelings create the signal that does the attracting! Coincidentally, these are the same ingredients that also make you a successful communicator using the Secret Language of Dogs. What you think and feel in every given moment is the frequency that the Universe (and your dog) is always responding to.

I meet a lot of interesting people, but this couple was definitely on the leading edge of thought creation. They told me that if they could maintain their presence and maximize their flow-state vibes, they would surely manifest the perfect dog for their lifestyle. Trust in the Universe is the final ingredient, they said.

I chuckled and reminded them that if they could maintain this level of presence when picking up the pup, then integrating them into their pack was going to be a piece of cake. I was both curious and excited to watch this adventure unfold. Would the Universe deliver them another match made in heaven?

## Letting Go of the Past

A few weeks later, Nikki received an email at 11:11 a.m. and had an unshakable hunch that this was the Universe delivering their request. They forwarded it to me so I could have a look. The message was from an elderly man who lived in an apartment on the waterfront. He was forthright and communicated that he suffered from sciatica and depression. He admitted that his dog had been extremely neglected for the better part of a year. The dog's name was Tiny Tim.

I studied his picture keenly. He was a 12–month-old toy-sized Yorkie. His hair was greasy, tangled, and knotted. A buildup of hardened black goop begged to be plucked from his eyes. I wasn't exactly sure how he could walk with those nails, either; they were so long they curved around in a circle. I exhaled and reminded myself that there was nothing serious going on here. A decent groomer could transform him in a few hours, and no one would remember Tiny Tim's past.

It's important that feelings of pity or judgments about an adopted dog's former life don't creep into your mindset. If they do, investigate it for only a little bit. Ask yourself why you're feeling sorry for a dog like Tiny Tim, but meditate for no longer than three minutes on these issues. Storylines like these can build up momentum in your psyche. Soon, they will take you into a place of toxic non-presence, and as such, will bring down your mood. Always remember, in the Secret Language of Dogs, feelings do all the communicating. When we feel sorry or angry, it makes our dogs feel concerned, nervous, or cautious. We can't project that if we want them to trust us, can we?

# The Art of Giving Space

Nikki and Rikki picked me up from the airport, and we drove directly to the old man's apartment to get their new dog. The couple's excitement was contagious but was also grounded and relaxed. Both women woke up earlier than usual to meditate and visualize the harmonious assimilation of their new pack. They also took Thelma and Louise for a longer-than-usual nature walk to drain them of their energy, in case they got anxious when left alone. Per my recommendation, they left the bulldogs crated until we arrived back with Tiny Tim. I assured them that the bulldogs would drift into a timeless vortex of relaxation, and that it would undoubtedly accelerate the integration phase later that afternoon.

We spent as little time as possible at the old man's apartment. We simply filled out the paperwork, made some pleasantries, then left. Tiny Tim shook nervously as we drove home. Rather than holding him or coddling him to soothe his nerves, I suggested that we place him on the floor between Rikki's feet. This is the posture of protection and can be studied further in Figure 15 at the end of this section. Puppies naturally angle themselves behind their moms in such a manner to make themselves feel safe. Our silence and actions allowed the Yorkie to process the situation for himself. Eventually, Tiny Tim calmed down and snuggled into Rikki's ankle. At this precise moment, I encouraged her to pick him up and place him on her lap. Of the many ways you can praise a dog, love always works best.

**Figure 15: Seated Posture of Protection**

We can use our body language, even while sitting, to communicate the feeling of safety to our dogs so that we can help them calm down and feel relaxed. Alternatively, the same position can be used to quell any anxiety or excitement our dog might be experiencing from a nearby distraction, such as a lively group of squirrels at the park.

When we place our dog between our legs, we are actually creating a physical and energetic barrier around their body. The position itself creates a little "dog den" for your dog to go in and chill out.

It's also an amazing position in which to meditate with your pet, because the intention of using Angle of Protection creates the emotion of tranquility within you.

# Fast Tracking the Integration Phase

I wasn't sure how Tiny Tim would react when he met Thelma and Louise. He couldn't have weighed more than five pounds soaking wet. Both bulldogs, at least when they were younger, could eat him for a snack if they wanted to. What I was certain of, however, is that the Yorkie would be much more at ease (and confident) if Thelma and Louise were relaxed and submissive when he first met them.

Thankfully, when we arrived at their house about 30 minutes later, we were well poised for a successful integration. Entering silently, we neither looked at the bulldogs nor acknowledged their presence. Alphas would never do that anyway. As a result of this, and my suggestion that they drape blankets three-quarters of the way down the sides of the crates, Thelma and Louise lay calmly with their chins on the floor. Dogs want to see what they can smell and sense from their crates. The blankets were a way of suggesting to the bulldogs that they ground their bellies on the earth.

Nikki and Rikki sensed some curiosity bubbling in Tiny Tim, and they wanted to let him explore. I advised against this. First, we needed to take an action that would establish that this was Peaceful Alpha territory to all the dogs in the pack. I encouraged Nikki to tie Tiny Tim's leash to the kitchen chair and give him some space to process the situation. As predicted, he started tugging on the leash and whining softly. What happened next was a delightful manifestation of my clients' desires.

The bulldogs, sensing Tiny Tim's anxiety, offered him some gestures of comfort. They started yawning and licking their lips to help him relax. The Yorkie caught these subtle Calming Signals in his peripheral vision and yawned himself as a social response to the group. Only a few moments later, he initiated his own Sequence of Surrender and sat down, eliminating any tension he had created on his own leash. Nikki, Rikki and I praised him softly but remained silent. We chose positions in the room that grouped the six of us into a semicircle, the shape of inclusion.

Tiny Tim let out a high-pitched squeal of a yawn and lay down. He rested his chin on his extra-small adorable front paws. After filling his belly with several calming breaths, he snorted the last of his resistance, then he licked his lips to make sure that the bulldogs didn't interpret his accidental eye contact as confrontational. Thelma and Louise responded by blinking at him (obviously, they preferred the laziest Calming Signal imaginable). This was the moment I was waiting for! The web of canine communication was forming, and bonding was taking place—not to mention, the vibes were incredibly tranquil.

The time was now ripe to encourage the dogs to freely interact with one another. I went to open crate doors while Rikki unleashed Tiny Tim. As Thelma and Louise casually walked toward the two women, they seemed to ignore the puppy completely. I explained to my clients that their furry gurus were doing this on purpose. Dogs greet one another by sniffing their rear ends. Allowing the smaller, younger dog to approach from the rear is simply a conscious expression of vulnerability. Thelma and Louise wanted Tiny Tim to feel comfortable in their home!

We hung out in the kitchen for about an hour before it was time for me to leave. As a finishing touch, I recommended that we do a small feeding ritual to complete the bonding process. I reached into my bag and pulled out three smoked sardine treats. I had Rikki place them in a bowl and claim them by standing over the top of them in the resource-guarding posture. The bulldogs slid their bottoms backward and lay down, while Tiny Tim trotted around them excitedly. Thelma looked at the Yorkie and yawned at him. She was telling him that no one eats until everyone is calm. Tiny Tim didn't hesitate to listen to his big sister and lay down several inches behind Thelma. We praised the pack as one unit, then calmly hand-fed them the treats.

## Transformation

One Sunday morning, a few weeks after our lesson, I received a short video message from Nikki and Rikki. The couple and their pack lounged comfortably on the king-sized bed. I could hear the Golden Girls snoring at the foot of the mattress. At first I couldn't see Tiny Tim, but then I found him curled up on Thelma's belly. His head was resting on her thigh, and he sported a new buzz cut. I barely recognized him with that bright red collar and bow tie of his!

"We've barely had to teach Tiny Tim anything," Rikki said. "Structure, repetition, and silence was our mantra for the first two days, then we basically just stopped trying anything, because he is so awesome! We knew that Thelma and Louise could do most of the training for us. We streamlined mealtimes. All dogs eat at the same time from separate bowls, and no dog eats until everyone is lying down. Tiny Tim already knows he's last in line. He waits, like, three inches behind the bulldogs and looks to them for everything. It's just so adorable. He's cunning and clever, and we just love how badass he thinks he is when he wants to wrestle with Thelma or Louise. Of course, they never lift a paw, but we're certain they find him as amusing as we do."

# Training Tips
## Rescue Dogs

1. Give your adopted dog space and silence to acclimate to your environment, and know that these are some of the highest expressions of love you can offer.

2. Be aware of your current emotional state and your intentions when adopting a dog. If it's to fill a void, perhaps caused by grief, loneliness, or sadness, do your best to be conscious of these feelings as you interact with your new dog.

3. Accelerate the acclimation period by creating a compassionate yet authoritative Peaceful Alpha first impression. Demonstrate control over the resources and territory early on and often.

4. Claim your new dog's food, treats, and toys as your own until they move through the Sequence of Surrender. This tip ensures that your dog will respect your authority on other issues.

5. Have clear routines for pee breaks, morning exercise, training time, and feeding schedules. This helps your dog predict how their days will unfold.

6. Have a clearly defined territory for your new dog to live, eat, and sleep in. Once your dog acclimates to these ground rules, you are welcome to expand the territory as they earn your trust.

# Meditation
## Building Trust with Touch

For this meditation you will need two leashes, a brush, a nail file, and relaxing music for your dog, such as nature sounds or binaural beats. Begin in an uncluttered space, and sit still, with your tools and your dog beside you.

Take 10 conscious breaths. Slowly leash your dog, and tether them to something in front of them. Form a lasso with the second leash, placing it around your dog's hindquarters, and fasten it to another fixture behind them. This gentle restraint will keep your furry guru standing still and safe. Now it's time to begin the working meditation of grooming your dog with love.

Gently run your hands along your dog's body. With mindful attention, feel for any lumps, bumps, ticks, or injuries. Focus on your dog's breath, and how they respond to your touch. If they enjoy something, give them a little more. If they startle or grimace, take note, and give the area of trauma or pain some space in order to earn their trust.

Next, gently cradle a hind leg and lift your dog's paw completely off the ground. Encourage your dog to trust you by putting weight into your hand before proceeding. Breathe. Gently file the nails of this paw and then repeat for each leg. Stay calm and project the vibe of tranquility. Do not get caught up in the actual results of the pedicure. Just ensure that your dog stays calm and relaxed. That is your focus. As you practice grooming your pet mindfully, they will learn to love this connection. Grooming, after all, is one of their primal needs.

To conclude the working meditation, use your nondominant hand, and fold your dog's hair upward while you softly brush it in smooth downward strokes. This ensures that the bristles reach the dog's skin and remove any unwanted undercoat. Work methodically along your dog's body. Take breaks if your dog is stressed, and always end on a positive note.

Complete the ritual by praising your dog, petting them, and giving them calm love. Clean your tools, and put them away with care so that they are ready when you next need them. This is the way of the Peaceful Alpha.

# 12

# How the Wise Feed Their Dogs

It was still dark outside, and Maddie wanted to fall back asleep. She meditated on the sound of the rain as it pelted the rooftop, hoping that might help her relax. Unfortunately, her attempt only lasted a moment before she lost her focus. Now she wondered whether it was time to take her cousin's puggle out for his morning business. Maddie glanced at the pillow beside her and sighed irritably. There he was again! Frustration crept in. How did he sneak into bed without her knowing?  No wonder she woke up early. The heat coming off his body was intense, but not as bad as the gas he passed during the night. *That can't be normal*, she thought.

Negative feelings about Kobe suddenly dominated her mind. *Be loving*, she told herself, as she took a deep breath. *He is adorable (at times), and a wonderful snuggler*, she reflected. Perhaps he would seem more charming if she wasn't still upset at him from the previous day.

It was only day three, and her house-sitting gig felt like she had bitten off more than she wanted to chew. Yesterday, Kobe opened the cupboard, pulled out a big bag of ketchup-flavored Doritos and trashed the pantry like a rock star. The day before that, Maddie found him standing on the kitchen counter staring her down. The brazen puggle was eating her fresh baguette and cold cuts. She had literally set them down a moment ago so she could go to the bathroom to wash her hands.

Unwilling to tolerate any more of his shenanigans, Maddie went online and began searching for solutions. She found my Facebook page and resonated with one of my posts, "Control the Resources to Control Your Dog." As luck would have it, I was already on the West Coast and happy to make a stop in Seattle to give her and Kobe a hand.

## The Need for Conscious Feeding

Maddie's cousin's one-story beach house looked cozy from the outside. Smoke was rising out of the chimney, and I could smell the dry cedar wood burning inside. Two puggle eyes watched my every step as I approached. I smiled, because Kobe seemed to protect his territory from the top of the couch. He looked so lazy and relaxed up there, which I liked. So far he seemed like a perfect dog to me. If he would only behave that way around food then we'd be set.

Maddie greeted me at the door, and we got right to the lesson. She was wondering how Kobe came to be so mischievous and asked me if I thought we could turn the situation around.

As far as the second part of her question went, I was optimistic that we would see a rapid transformation in Kobe. Considering Maddie had only been living with him for three days, she had a tremendous advantage over many people in similar situations. Kobe wasn't a reflection of her; he was a product of his lifestyle with her cousin. Once Maddie demonstrated some control over the resources in her territory, I was confident that Kobe would naturally become calm and obedient. To him, it would simply be a situation of understanding the limits and expectations that his new master communicated. Dogs live in the now and are capable of transforming instantly. That's what makes them our furry gurus.

As far as her first question, I believed that his mischievous personality had blossomed rather innocently. Many dogs discover how to manipulate their owners into giving them food without us even realizing it. It happens all the time, even when we think it's something we would never do. The issue with feeding your dog on their terms, and not yours, is that they come to discover that they have control over the resources. This means that they have control over you. That's why you feed them when they whine, bark, or give you those irresistible "puppy eyes" at the table. Obviously, this taxes your Peaceful Alpha power heavily.

## Don't Be So Easily Manipulated

To illustrate to Maddie how clever and manipulative some dogs can be around food, I told her a story about a golden retriever I once saw at an outdoor coffee shop. She roamed from person to person, stopping in front of those who were eating baked goods, breakfast sandwiches, and other various treats. I was astonished at how easily the dog could sense which people would be willing to share their food with her and which wouldn't. Then I remembered how emotionally sensitive canines are.

The golden retriever actually zeroed in on the patrons who were happy, joyful, or relaxed. She would sit in front of them and flash a smile as she offered an unsolicited paw to shake. If they ignored this cute and seemingly innocent routine, she would let out a quiet little whine and wave her paw more vigorously to get their attention. At this point, she'd already be drooling (an obvious conditioned response to human food). Astoundingly, many people not only fed her, they seemed to take joy in it. They would praise her and take her picture, not realizing their participation only served to reinforce her cycle of manipulation.

Maddie laughed out loud when I told her this. She remembered watching her cousin feed Kobe all kinds of people food when he was a puppy. In fact, she was pretty sure the puggle didn't know what actual dog food even tasted like anymore. She had been cooking him potatoes, carrots, chicken, and eggs because there was no kibble in the house, nor a dog bowl in sight. If Kobe's diet was mostly human food at this point, which it likely was, Maddie wondered if that would contribute to his mischievousness? Aside from giving him a little gas and potentially lacking in optimal canine nutrients I didn't think it really mattered, one way or the other.

## The Myth about People Food

A dog's behavior around food is not a reflection of *what* they eat; it's a product of how they were *allowed* to eat. Since dogs don't speak English, how can they tell the difference between food that is marketed for you and food that is marketed for them?

Canines don't differentiate in this regard. In general, if their nose suggests an object is desirable, they will want to eat it. This might explain why some canines forage through the trash can only to consume things like used tissues or feminine hygiene products, or continuously eat their own feces, even though it actually gives them diarrhea!

I'm not trying to make your stomach turn; I'm simply trying to highlight some basic canine motivation so that you can be a better Peaceful Alpha for your dog. Maddie blushed when I told her this. It's as if I was reading her mind, and I already knew the big secret. It turns out that Kobe was a trash-eater as well.

## Mastery over Resources

When any food is in sight, a Peaceful Alpha expects their dog to behave like a fly on the wall. That means the dog is calm, relaxed, and at ease, knowing that they can't consume it unless given permission. When a dog is hawking you for some of your food, or they are already deep in the act of begging (which is really just an expression of overexcitement), engaging with them directly only intensifies their energy.

"Is that why Kobe becomes even more obnoxious when I yell at him to go away?" Maddie asked.

"Of course it is," I replied. "There's an easy way to train him to leave you alone. You simply need to teach him that you're never going to share with him. The boundary you're establishing is that when you eat, you eat in peace. The way to accomplish this is to simply turn your back on him and eat in silence. Anytime he changes the angle, keep pivoting and turning your back. Eventually he will exhaust himself and learn he can no longer manipulate you. This is the beginning of Kobe entering the Sequence of Surrender. Wait for him to place his chin on the floor and then praise him softly. That will show Kobe you're deeply in tune with him, even though your back is turned."

# Lessons from an Opportunistic Guru

I tend to have a special place in my heart for dogs like Kobe; they offer us a variety of life lessons worth examining. I could hardly blame him for sneaking into a warm bed or snacking on human delicacies, nor could I find fault with his resource-guarding issues, for they were all cultivated in the garden of human naiveté. To his way of thinking, those cold cuts on the counter were sent to him from heaven . . . okay, perhaps that's debatable, but he acted as if they were. That's what I want to focus on for just a moment.

Let me remind you that the Universe is always delivering our desires. It wants us to have what we want. The question is, do you recognize your manifestations when they arrive, or do you hesitate to take action? Do you feel that you deserve them, or do you sabotage yourself with thoughts of self-doubt?

Feelings like "This is too good to be true" tend to surface quite often in our culture. The issue with this belief patterning is that it is fear-based and takes us out of the flow state (the place Peaceful Alphas always want to be). It's also worth remembering: Alphas never hesitate in nature, nor do they feel guilty. If and when they do, they lose all of their power. Let that thought marinate.

# A Word on Dog Food

A lot of my clients seem to be confused and anxious about what to feed their dog, when to feed them, and how much to feed them. Some people look for recipes online and cook for their canine. Others go to the butcher and feed their dog raw meat. Still others have all different kinds of kibble. Some have grains; some don't. Some contain small proteins, such as fish or chicken; others more exotic options like bison or kangaroo. We also have what veterinary science asks us to consider. They guide you into believing that your dog should eat kibble of a certain shape or size specific to your breed. Alternatively, they may have you believing that the only thing your dog can thrive on is their medicated canned food.

With so many options to choose from today, it can be more than a little overwhelming for dog owners. The pet industry has the second highest profit margins next to the pharmaceutical industry (who do you think supplies the vets with their food?). Their marketing is about putting pressure on dog owners, because fear has proven to be the best marketing tactic—big business capitalizes on the fact that your concerns are coming from a place of pure intent.

People want to do their best. In that light, I wanted to remind readers that dog food as you know it didn't even exist 100 years ago. Feeding your dog three times a day, much as you would feed yourself, is also a product of marketing. The only reason we believe this is the best way to eat is because big business wins when we follow this route, and we end up consuming more than we need.

The main point here is that fear and anxiety around what and when to feed your dog only serves to take away your Peaceful Alpha power, and we can't allow that to happen. There is really no right or wrong way on this topic. Whatever you're feeding your pooch, and however often you do it, just do it calmly. Put their food in a clean bowl, and place it on the floor. Claim the bowl as yours until your dog fully surrenders. That's all you need to do to be a Peaceful Alpha. Don't worry about the other stuff.

# Transformation

I swung back to Maddie's cabin a week later and brought lunch for the two of us. I wanted to see firsthand how Kobe would react around food. Even though he smelled our tuna sandwiches, I was pleasantly surprised to see that he remained perched on the top of his couch and hardly moved a muscle.

"Oh, don't even worry about him," Maddie said. "I ignored him for three straight days, and he eventually realized that I was never going to share with him. I also put baby locks on the cupboards and keep the trash in the garage. I've become the total boss of this territory," Maddie smiled at me. "Why don't you sit with Kobe and let me plate this for us."

"I went to the pet store and bought Kobe some premium kibble," Maddie continued, while she poured him a bowl and placed it on the counter beside our sandwiches. "Alright boys, you can come to the table now," she commanded us softly.

On that note, Kobe jumped down and trotted into the kitchen obediently. I was intrigued and followed quietly.

Maddie placed his bowl on the ground and told him, "Wait." Once Maddie and I sat down, she said to Kobe, "Go ahead." As he started eating, Maddie took a bite and looked at me with a funny expression. "What are you waiting for? Dig in. A pack should eat together." I laughed and took a bite.

"I had no idea Kobe could be such a good boy, Jesse. I think I'll let him in the bed tonight." I caught Maddie smiling as she glanced at Kobe to make sure he was behaving, which he was indeed.

# Training Tips
## Feeding Your Dog

1. If you're unsure about what to feed your dog, don't cook for it. Experiment with different options that fit your budget and please your dog's palate. You will be at ease knowing your dog is receiving all the essential vitamins and minerals required for their health.

2. Train your dog's digestive system to take in one big meal a day. Fasting is natural for all animals (and humans) and keeps the body healthy. The side benefit is that it's easier to pick up one big poop a day as opposed to three small ones.

3. Allow 60 minutes of rest after eating before doing anything vigorous with your dog. This prevents the risk of their stomach flipping, which is a painful and risky situation requiring immediate veterinary attention.

4. Eat your meals at the same time you feed your dog. A pack that eats together is happy together.

5. Eat with your back slightly turned away from your dog so it can be peaceful and relaxed. Alphas don't watch others eat; it sends the wrong message.

6. Keep your dog's food bowl clean and off the floor when it's not mealtime. This allows you to bring your attention and care to the vessel you use to feed your dog and also gives you Peaceful Alpha power by keeping the "resources scarce."

7. When presenting your dog with their food, claim it first as a "power object." Once your dog is fully surrendered, reward them by letting them eat.

# Meditation

## Bringing Calmness to Mealtime

This mealtime meditation ritual will deepen your connection with your dog while you simultaneously develop your Peaceful Alpha power. Begin by preparing your own meal mindfully. Pay attention to any hunger impulses or temptations you may experience as you plate your food. Arrange your food so that it looks beautiful—this is an act of love for yourself—then set your plate aside on the counter.

As you do this, glance at your dog, and hold eye contact with them for a moment, then blink, or do a micro-yawn. This sequence of communication reminds your dog that you are aware of them watching you. The intention is to activate their Sequence of Surrender while you relate to food.

Dogs like to eat as a pack. Pick up your dog's empty bowl from the floor. This will have your dog calm and totally focused on you. Fill up their bowl with kibble and then place it on the floor. Stand tall. This is your focus as you stand directly over the top of your dog's food, communicating that you're claiming this resource. Now ease off the intensity of your body language. Be in harmony with your dog's emotion. When your dog is lying with their chin down on the floor, tell them, "Okay," and slide the bowl toward them.

Now eat your meal as your dog eats theirs. Keep your back turned, but keep your ears tuned in to your dog. This is the meditation. Nothing else exists right now. Simply eat your meal. Pay attention to the sensations of taste, texture, smell, and flavor. When you learn how to focus on these while still listening to your dog eat, inner peace will already be pooling within your presence.

# 13

# Puppyhood 101
## Teach Them When They Are Young

Joseph was in a pinch. He found me on the internet and reached out. Two months ago, he and his wife Miriam were on top of the world. While celebrating Miriam's big promotion over dinner, Joseph, a trust-your-gut kind of guy, made two impulsive decisions that Miriam wholeheartedly supported. The first was that he would quit his boring desk job, work from home, and finally launch that internet business he felt passionate about. The second was to purchase a puppy. When Miriam transitioned into longer hours at the office, the dog would provide wonderful companionship for Joseph.

Several days later, Joseph came home with Rambo, an eight-week-old male rottweiler puppy. Within weeks of canine ownership, though, the couple's emotional high had quickly become an "oy vey!" scenario.

Joseph was calm with me on the phone, but his tone was soft and devoid of all emotion. He said night-times were exhausting. No one, including Rambo, slept a wink. Aggravating the situation further, potty training had become a nightmare. Joseph had caught himself screaming at Rambo after repeatedly stepping on landmines of poop. And the young rottie had chewed through multiple sets of Miriam's pantyhose, work shoes, and purses.

I felt that I could bring ease into Joseph and Miriam's lives by offering them some simple, commonsense approaches to early puppyhood the Peaceful Alpha way. That's why I hopped on a plane immediately and flew to Brooklyn.

## Even the Young Have Lessons to Teach Us

When I pulled my rental car up the driveway, I noticed that Joseph and Miriam lived in a cute little bungalow. Walking toward their door, I counted no less than six pee pads scattered randomly across the planks of their wooden porch. Most were soiled yellow from day-old urine. There were also some puppy turds on the wood.

I didn't judge because I've seen this so many times before. The logic goes something like this: if you put down lots of targets, surely your dog will hit them. In reality, potty training doesn't work that way at all. In fact, by not keeping the area clean, it effectively communicates to Rambo that the porch is a latrine.

Before ringing the bell, I kissed my fingers and touched the Jewish mezuzah on the upper right side of their door. Joseph greeted me a few moments later with a warm smile and a velvety black kippa on his head. He had massive bags under his eyes, and his breath smelled like black coffee. Miriam stood behind him, arms crossed, toes tapping anxiously. As they welcomed me into their home, Miriam suggested that I keep my shoes on because the floor was disgusting (a reference to the frequency of potty accidents). I followed them into the kitchen, where I noticed a shredded roll of paper towel on the counter. It rested on the ledge beside a chewed-up bottle of urine cleaner and a box of fresh pee pads. This couple was right in the thick of the intense puppy days that most dog owners forget ever happened.

Rambo was lying on the kitchen floor with his back turned to us. Snoring deeply, he looked adorable as he bathed in the warm patch of sun. Humans and animals have different relationships with the sun. We tend to fear it as a source of cancer creation, yet nature tends to worship it, relax into it, and use it for healing nourishment. I have no doubt that Rambo chose that spot on purpose. It gave him a feeling of comfort and tranquility. The young furry guru was already offering a lesson: we would be wise to revere the sun for its nourishing power, and perhaps show it a little gratitude.

## All You Need to Know about Potty Training

I broke the ice by suggesting that we address the potty-training situation and clean it up immediately (no pun intended). Miriam smiled, and with the zeal of an experienced lawyer, asked me how I proposed we do that.

I explained that Rambo just wanted to please his masters. That meant that all we needed to do was communicate to him where we wanted his latrine to be. Naturally, we would use the territory and a few other nonverbal methods to accomplish this feat efficiently. With consistency and presence, I knew the potty-training issue would resolve itself in a matter of days.

I first suggested that they identify a clear territory where they want their dog to pee and poo (not the front porch!). I recommend making the target a stone garden or a discrete patch of dirt in the corner of their yard, rather than allowing Rambo to "go" anywhere on the grass. Most people don't realize the yellowing effects that dog pee has on plant life until it's too late to reverse it.

The smartest and fastest way to establish this behavior is to carry the puppy to the designated target first thing in the morning, upon waking from a nap, or a few minutes after a meal. In these scenarios, you can typically expect your pup to pee within seconds of placing it down. When they do, offer them love (soft verbal praise) and/or a highly motivating treat, such as a piece of cheese, kosher salami, something from the pet store, and so on.

Practicing this for a couple of days will teach your dog that going to the bathroom on this spot earns a response that feels good to them. Obviously, they will want to repeat this over and over.

# Mastery of Territory

Now that you've communicated where you want your dog to go to the bathroom, the next step is to govern your territory like a Peaceful Alpha. This means staying present and catching your dog in the exact moment it makes an accident indoors. Take a peek at Figure 16 to get a sense of what this nonverbal communication looks like. It's so simple, but very powerful. I also recommend getting rid of the pee pad method (indoors and on the porch) and switching to a "confine the territory method."

It was much easier to supervise Rambo when he was contained in the kitchen, as opposed to giving him free rein in the house. When he proved that he could be accident-free for a few days, then we rewarded him by giving him more space. If not, we gave him less. Adjusting the territory like this sends a very clear message to the canine: Don't soil my house!

By bringing this level of awareness to the places you choose to rest in any environment, you build tremendous Peaceful Alpha power. The reason for this is layered. First, it demonstrates that you have your pack's emotional well-being at heart. Second, and perhaps of more importance, it puts you into a position where you can operate proactively. The swiftness and timing of your actions are communications.

**Figure 16: Mastery of Territory**

Wherever you sit in your environment should be a conscious decision. You should choose to sit in that particular spot on purpose. This is what your dog does.

Ask yourself this: When you rest, can you see your entire territory? If not, you're not living up to your Peaceful Alpha potential from your dog's perspective.

Remember: the windows, the doorway, and the hallway are the access points into your territory. These are places that your dog will feel need watching.

# Dealing with Potty Accidents When They Occur

Using the Secret Language of Dogs offers the fastest way to nip potty accidents in the bud. I like to describe the following method as "good cop/bad cop."

A word of caution: Pay attention to your pup's Calming Signals to make sure that you're in tune with your energetic intensities. Stay present. Have an awareness of your dog in each moment, as if you were an eagle surveying the forest. Remember, they will never want to be apart from you, so when they inevitably leave the room, chances are high that they have to go to the bathroom and don't want you to know. Being aware of this cue allows you to take your dog outside to the target.

If your puppy goes potty indoors, and you don't catch it in the moment, shame on you. Dogs are present-moment beings. Thus showing anger after the moment has occurred is foolish; it is a reactionary response and creates fear, while draining you of your Peaceful Alpha power.

An eagle can swoop down and catch prey when it least expects it, so be like the eagle, and catch your dog in the moment it makes an indoor potty. In this moment, snap your fingers or make a gentle conflict-seeking sound, followed by direct eye contact. This action is the "bad cop" moment, and the Forbidden Angle clearly communicates "no." Don't feel sad or think your puppy will get mad at you. Remember, fear is a normal emotion, and animals don't relate to it like we do.

Next, quickly approach your dog, scoop them up, and instantly transform your energy into love. Angling their head away from your face helps to keep them calm and allows them to see where you're taking them. Carry them to the designated outdoor pee spot, and go through the ritual of waiting for them to do their business, praising them, and so on. This step is the "good cop," and it completes the communication directive. Now your pup knows two things: peeing inside is bad, and peeing outside is good.

The last piece of the potty-training puzzle, and probably the most difficult one for people to do, is to put your dog on a consistent rhythm and stick to it. Since Joseph was going to be working from home, I recommended that he take Rambo out every 90 minutes, on the clock, for the next 10 days. This is more than enough time to potty-train a puppy. In fact, I was pretty sure that they would start seeing results within 48 hours.

# Embracing a Puppy's Need to Chew

Joseph, Miriam, and I had been sitting at the table discussing the potty-training situation for nearly 20 minutes. Rambo was so quiet I almost forgot that he was sleeping like a baby. When he finally woke up, he shuffled his way toward me and nose-kissed my ankle to say hi. He then settled between Miriam's feet and lay back down. With comedic timing (for me, not for my clients), Rambo began nibbling Miriam's leather moccasins. This segued perfectly into our next topic: how to stop Rambo from destroying her favorite items.

Before tackling the how, let's quickly understand the why. Puppies chew things to explore, learn, and soothe the pain of teething. How we react in these moments shapes their future behavior. Screaming or showing excitement, for example, quickly turns the act of teething into an interactive game. On the other hand, acting assertively and using Alpha tactics to guard the moccasin like a resource (a power object) would effectively stop Rambo from chewing them.

Asserting yourself in this fashion to such a young pup, however, makes you come across as unnecessarily scary. It's not appropriate until the dog is about six months of age. A more gentle and effective solution to solving a puppy's teething needs is to simply acknowledge that they have them. Miriam's shoes, pantyhose, and other possessions smell like love to Rambo; her scent is what magnetizes his attention toward her possessions. Rather than blaming the puppy for nibbling on them, I suggested a simple bait-and-switch tactic.

Rubber KONGs and rubber chew toys that can be stuffed with food are essential items for early puppyhood. I have found that smearing some peanut butter or cream cheese into these toys, then freezing them, makes them even more enticing for canines, because they last longer and the cold soothes their gums. Consumables like bully sticks, dehydrated sweet potato, or elk antlers are enchanting distractions. For a pup with teething needs, a satiating chew treat becomes a play activity that leaves them feeling relaxed and tranquil. The next time Rambo got into one of Miriam's belongings, I suggested that she offer him a high-value chew. Doing so would communicate, "Chew this, not that." In a short period of time, the Law of Attraction would simply guide Rambo toward the more satisfying choice.

# Teaching Your Puppy to Sleep through the Night

Miriam knew that Rambo would grow into a 90-pound dog one day. Who could blame her for not wanting him to take over their bed? As it was, my client's living room now resembled that of a college dormitory: Rambo's crate was in the center of the room, angled toward the head of the couch, which was made up like a makeshift bed. The coffee table was cluttered with Joseph's sleeping meds and foam ear plugs.

Both Miriam and Joseph knew that sleeping on the sofa wasn't the best option for their relationship, but it was a necessary sacrifice in order for the couple to catch up on some much-needed sleep. As a result, they felt more disconnected from one another than they ever had. Romance had completely vanished; grumpiness and edginess had ensued.

Establishing some rules and expectations around sleeping through the night are part of the package of being a Peaceful Alpha. As the master of your territory, it's up to you to communicate where you want your dog to sleep. Keep in mind that it's not really natural for a dog to sleep on its own, away from the pack. This partially explains why Rambo was wailing and whining at night. The other part of the explanation is that dogs communicate using emotions. The clever pup had already figured out that Joseph was a little soft-hearted. A little cry meant that Joseph would let him out of the crate and bring him into the bed.

I recommended that Joseph move back into the bedroom immediately. I also recommended that the couple place the crate under the kitchen table, a spot where Rambo had already revealed that he felt safe resting. My clients liked the idea but resisted it slightly because they believed Rambo would cry forever. Of course he would cry, I validated to them, but he would stop quickly when he realized that they were not going to come downstairs and let him out of the crate. I was prepping my clients to shift into a gentle puppy Ferberization (a sleep-training technique that is effective in teaching human babies to become calm when separated from their mothers), if you will.

It's really important to harmonize your puppy with your desired sleep patterns. Instead of adapting to the wailing puppy, remain stoic, and expect that they will adapt to you, because they will, I promise. The strategies of a Peaceful Alpha are born directly from nature, and nature is often ruthless from an emotional standpoint. Birds kick their young out of the nest, and due to harsh living environments or scarce food supply, many other animals abandon their young to survive on their own; thus, asking your dog to sleep in the kitchen in a crate really isn't that bad, even if it means a night or two of crying and a potentially soiled crate once or twice.

There are a few other ways you can bring ease to your puppy in these times and accelerate the transition. The first is to bring warmth into the crate. The second is to bring your scent into the crate. The third is to make the crate feel like a den by putting a blanket over the top. Wrapping a hot water bottle in a stinky t-shirt usually does the trick. In order to bring ease to your ears, you can also play some white noise or nature sounds, which will act as a bit of natural lullaby for your dog to relax to.

To summarize the game plan for my clients, I suggested they take Rambo out for a pee break before they go to bed themselves. No matter the circumstances, I also urged them to leave Rambo in there all night long. In the morning, when they awoke, they should immediately go to his crate and take him to his designated potty spot. My clients agreed to give it a shot. They knew that the first night or two might be messy, and not just in an emotional kind of way, but they were excited about the rapid adjustment and ease that it would bring into their life.

# Transformation

Two weeks later, I hopped on a video call with Joseph to check on their progress. He was in the kitchen. His face looked clear, and the whites of his eyes shone with a calm, clear-headed energy. Obviously the household was getting its sleep again!

After exchanging some greetings, Joseph flipped the angle of his screen and showed me Rambo. The pup was now much bigger, and he was just waking up from a nap in his crate. Draped in a brown flannel sheet, the crate was discretely camouflaged under the kitchen table. Joseph opened the metal gate without a sound. In a relaxed voice he said, "Potty time, dude." A few moments later, I heard the chime of a bell. It hung on the glass sliding door that led into the backyard. Clever, I reflected. The bell was fastened at the perfect height for Rambo's nose.

I watched Rambo trot proudly after his master. Joseph was so confident that he let his pup go outside while he remained standing in the kitchen. Rambo squatted on all fours. He tinkled on a dirt patch beside a big tree in the corner of the yard. "Attaboy!" Joseph applauded proudly as he jingled a tin full of dehydrated liver treats. The sound, smell, and love in Joseph's voice urged Rambo into a full-out gallop back toward the house. When the puppy got close to the door, Joseph tossed a healthy-sized treat on the floor inside the kitchen to guide the puppy well inside. Without talking to or touching his dog, Joseph placed a bully stick on the floor. Rambo thumped his belly onto the floor, and placed one paw on his high-value chew. Then he gnawed his way into heaven.

Joseph thanked me. "Jesse, these little suggestions you offered really got us on track. Rambo is an awesome, calm little dude. We just love him." Then he winked at me and said, "Miriam is very thankful as well. Next time you're out this way, you have to come for a visit."

# Training Tips
## Puppyhood

1. Staring at your dog—for example, while you're waiting for it to make a pee—sends them a mixed message. Your unconscious use of the Forbidden Angle suggests to your puppy that you feel it is doing something wrong.

2. As a general rule, try to open your angle of observation to 45 degrees. This gesture gives your dog space and ease to explore, play, and go to the bathroom. Think of this action as consciously creating the vibration of tranquility. Doing this on purpose cultivates Peaceful Alpha power.

3. Hang a bell on the door you most commonly use to take your dog out to pee, and ring it every time you go out. Eventually, the bell will ring when you least expect it. When you hear it, immediately praise your pup and take them outside.

4. Puppies have a strong need to chew. Embrace it. Stuffing a rubber chew toy with peanut butter or cream cheese, then freezing it, turns the natural need for chewing into an incredibly satiating activity for a teething puppy. Keep a few of these in the freezer, so you have one ready to go anytime you need it.

# Meditation

## Cultivating Peaceful Alpha Power

Before you begin this meditation, gather some of the power objects your puppy chews on that you don't want it to, items such as shoes, socks, pantyhose, and so on. Hold them in your lap, and take a resting position (in a chair or on the floor). Track the peak of your exhales, and try to count 10 of them in a row. Let us begin a meditative training exercise that will establish you as the "all seeing" Peaceful Alpha. At least your puppy will think this, and with this power, establishing rules and boundaries in any given moment will become effortless.

From your resting position, stand up slowly. Start to zen-walk into another room. Bring your attention to all of your senses. Feel your feet on the floor, and move with the grace of a panther. Don't look back at your pup. Alphas never look back. Instead, listen. What does it sound like when your puppy stands up? When it inevitably follows you, does it trot or does it walk? Focus all of your senses into the things that are happening within your territory.

Walk past a mirror, fridge, or TV, and drop the power object but do not look at it. Instead, continue flowing slowly, but watch your puppy through the reflection. If your puppy so much as even puts their nose on it, pivot and stare. The Forbidden Angle in this precise moment can be gentle, but don't underestimate its potency. Watch for a Calming Signal, pivot back, and continue walking. Keep your attention on your puppy using the reflection. Practice this for a  few days with various power objects. Your puppy will soon believe that you have eyes in the back of your head, and that all power objects flow through you.

# 14

# Children as Peaceful Alphas

Stacey, a commercial real estate agent in Michigan, was an incredibly busy single mother. Yet she woke up early every morning to make breakfast for her 12-year-old son William, then packed his lunch while he walked their mostly majestic husky before school. After work, she'd come home, make dinner, and help William with his homework. When she'd finally get William and his beloved husky to bed (together), she'd find time to exercise, meditate, and journal before finally hitting the sack. Though she was extremely busy, she prided herself on raising an independent son who was responsible and trustworthy enough to look after their dog.

Stacey had worked through the grief of losing her husband and had finally moved on in life. In fact, she had recently met someone really nice, whom she adored. His name was Ted. He was an engineer at the automotive plant and a total gentleman.

His only downside was that he wasn't much of a dog guy. Ted's first visit to the house was horrific. Wanting to make a good impression he exuberantly greeted Fang at the door. What a total miscalculation. The white husky growled loudly, bounded right for him, then pounced on his chest. Ted left, horrified and embarrassed.

Stacey contacted me a few days later. Though she was a little distraught, she had the clarity to know it was time to deal with Fang's issues. I was very happy to cross the border and head to Michigan.

# Children, Empathy, and Intuition

My knock on Stacey's door triggered a single deep bark, but I felt oddly at ease. There was no stress in Fang's notification. She was simply alerting her masters, saying "We have a visitor." Furthermore, my ears told me that the dog was quite far from the door, and I sensed that she wasn't bounding toward the entrance to protect her territory.

A moment later the door swung open.

"Hey, Jesse," Stacey greeted me warmly and invited me inside. She was wearing a cool citrine necklace, the crystal for personal power and healthy boundaries. I suddenly had a great vibe for how the lesson would unfold.

"Make yourself at home," she said, after I caught myself wiping husky hair off her mail-desk and placing my keys down.

My eyes started scanning their territory. The wooden floor was scratched up from Fang's nails. There also seemed to be an endless amount of chew ropes lying around, making it logical to deduce that a significant level of indoor play occurred in this hallway. I peeked into the living room and noticed that William had Fang restrained on a leash.

The thin leather leash was well worn and connected to a light-weight nylon bridle that was attached to her snout. Though she stood in the protective angle in front of her young master, the leash was droopy and tension-free. Fang's tail was wagging rapidly. Her pure white coat and hypnotic green eyes looked spectacular, but it was her energy that made her majestic. She was pure tranquility and love, at least in this moment.

Who says children can't be Peaceful Alphas? They have such a wonderful ability to focus their attention, they basically live in the flow state and their intuitions are wide open. In many respects, the work of a Peaceful Alpha is to remember how to be more childlike in their dog's presence.

I asked William what he thought his dog was feeling right now. With quiet confidence, he told me that she was getting excited and that she wanted to meet me. On that cue, Fang whined and inched herself forward. I noticed William struggling to stay anchored on his spot, though he did. The tightness on her leash was making him feel unsure of himself, so I started to coach him a little.

"The best way to calm dogs down when they are too excited is to speak to them using actions not words. She wants to meet me, but meeting me will only make her rambunctious. That's why you have her leashed. Think of an action that you can make that conveys the message 'You're not meeting him now!'"

William stayed silent, but I could see that a light bulb was going off inside his head. He led Fang farther away from me, walking her into the kitchen. Without needing to teach him, he already had an inclination of how to deal with power objects (things that magnetize our dog's attention). "Excellent," I praised William and caught him revealing a tiny smile. Children are so clever and naturally in tune with their dogs. When we learn to trust them with some basic responsibilities (like feeding, training, and exercising the dog), they tend to do it with more focus, calmness, and compassion than we do. No wonder Fang and her master were so connected.

## The Kung Fu Finger/Tailbone Combo

William led his husky away from me, but it was clear that she was still feeling some excitement, so I made the following suggestion: "Instead of petting Fang to calm her down, I want you to make your index finger feel like a pencil. Gently put pressure on the top of her neck with your nail. This is called Kung Fu Finger."

Fang had never felt this style of touch from her humans before. She immediately glanced at William, wondering what he wanted, while offering him a lip-lick and a nervous scratch of her ear with her hind leg.

"Cool. Now you've got her focused on you, and not on me," I said. "To Fang, Kung Fu Finger feels like the tooth of another dog. You can use it in a moment like this to communicate your desire for her to calm down. Think of it translating into directives like 'No,' 'Settle down,' 'Stop,' and 'Chill out.' It's an entirely natural experience in her world."

William broke his silence and asked me what to do next. "Move your Kung Fu Finger from the nape of her neck to her tailbone," I said. "Now you're telling her to stay put."

The downward pressure on her tailbone was enough to prompt Fang into the Sequence of Surrender. In a matter of seconds, she went from standing to sitting to lying down with her chin on the floor. William intuitively stroked Fang's ears and told her she was a good girl. Stacey looked pretty impressed with her son's ability to command his husky with love and respect.

So far so good, I thought.

## Dogs and Your Inner Child

"You like to play with Fang using these ropes, don't you?" I asked, as I pointed to one of the tug toys on the floor. William's face lit up with excitement.

"Oh, yes!" exclaimed Stacey. "We both do. That's how we exercise her."

Thoughts create feelings, a quantum field our dogs are viscerally immersed within. Suddenly, the expressive husky raised her nose to the sky. Vibing off the excitement of her pack, she let out a cute howl, which then turned into a yawn. The Calming Signal was an attempt to transition smoothly from her state of tranquility into the sudden surge of joy. What a guru!

Nothing brings out a human's inner child more than playing with their dog. All dog owners know this. I've seen grown men, executives of some pretty serious corporations, who turn into seven-year-olds at the dog park. The feelings evoked from playtime are a gateway directly into the flow state (which is precisely where Peaceful Alphas aspire to remain). Yet playtime with our dogs is often one-sided and unconscious, leading to all kinds of behavioral issues that we fail to consider, like jumping, biting, barking and scratching. I took a moment to myth-bust the idea that playing with a dog is, in fact, not great exercise at all.

Canines have limitless reserves of physical energy. They can literally run all day long! Thus, physical exercise on its own rarely brings our pups into the desired state of calmness we crave. In fact, it can often wind the dog up even more, making playing a one-way ticket into overexcitement. The best thing about play is that it's motivating for many dogs. We can use our dog's motivation to play as a way of sharpening their focus, which in turn, calms them down significantly. Our emotional state, tone of voice, and most importantly, the boundaries we set when playing are what make us a Peaceful Alpha.

"May I please watch how you play with Fang?" I asked William.

"Okey-dokey," he responded shyly.

William unclipped Fang's Gentle Leader head collar and calmly dropped her leash to the ground. The furry guru didn't move. She continued lying on the floor, focused intently on her young master as he walked toward a well-frayed rope toy.

In the past few moments, William had been relating to Fang with the Kung Fu Finger, and his calm actions had given him an accumulation of Peaceful Alpha power. That's why Fang was so chilled out. She remained casually lying on her spot as he walked away. I chuckled, wondering to myself what was about to happen next.

"Who wants to play? Who wants to play?" William's pre-teen tone was squeaky, enthusiastic, and high-pitched.

As I had expected, Fang bolted vigorously toward him. Instinctively, William held the toy high above his head and the husky jumped up repeatedly for it. William appeared to be playing some kind of keep-away game with his dog, and I cringed.

"Okay, stop!" I exclaimed. "Turn your back to her immediately, drop the toy, and ignore your dog."

Fang understood the message before my clients. The most gentle way to train any canine to stop jumping is to calmly offer them your back. It's what any mother animal in nature would do to gently disengage herself from that kind of aggressive (and playful) energy. Animal parents don't play with their young like we play with our dogs; it sends the wrong message. Animal parents have authority and responsibility. It doesn't mean they don't play; they just play and teach at the same time. Peaceful Alphas do the same, even if they are children. That is the responsibility of the human in this relationship.

After William had offered Fang his back, the dog yawned and backed up a step. Her head was curiously cocked to the side, sensing something different was up, though she was still focusing intently on the toy in William's hand.

"Slowly turn and face your dog," I coached. "Place the toy between your feet. This is the Asset Ownership posture. Good. Now stare at Fang a moment, and wait," I said.

Fang moaned and went through the Sequence of Surrender once more. When we relate to Power Objects the way one dog would to another (by hovering over them in the Asset Ownership posture and engaging in the Forbidden Angle), our dogs naturally yield. It doesn't mean they are sad. It just means that they respect our authority and know to surrender.

"Excellent," I said. "Now reward that awesome behavior by playing with her, but do so at a much calmer level to reinforce the new boundary. Think 3 out of 10 on the 'excitement meter' instead of 10 out of 10."

William understood my directive. He sat down on the floor in front of Fang and silently offered her the rope. The two of them tugged gently back and forth. All too often, people tend to make their dogs way too hyper when they play with them. No wonder Fang responded excitedly to Stacey's friend Ted—his enthusiasm was what Fang was conditioned to respond to. Naturally she bounded toward him and jumped and scratched.

# Transformation

Stacey and I did a follow-up video conference about 21 days after my visit. It was more than enough time for my clients to form the conscious habit of playing with awareness and teaching. Stacey was very grateful for our coaching session. Simply offering Fang their backs when she was excited and channeling her focus during playtime turned her into a deeply calm and joyful dog. William was just getting back from a long after-school walk with his husky. I watched him use the Kung Fu Finger on her tailbone to get her to sit immediately after coming inside the house. He unclipped the leash and hung it up, then he commanded Fang to "Stay" while he casually walked toward a rope toy.

"Is that Jesse on the computer? Watch this Jesse," he said. "I'm going to hide this toy, then I'm going to tell Fang to go find it, then she will bring it to me, and we will play a light game of tug-o-war." I beamed with pride alongside Stacey.

While the boy and his dog were playing quietly in the background, Stacey told me that Fang had really blossomed into a calm and trustworthy dog. Fang was no longer "mostly majestic"; she was "awesome." In fact, she had even stopped shedding as much.

I explained that when dogs get very excited (or nervous), their skin tightens and this causes them to shed more. Then she lowered her voice and told me that even Ted likes Fang now. He started coming over to the house again and was very impressed with William's ability to handle her. The best part? When Ted ignores Fang, she just lies at his feet. I got off the call with a huge smile.

# Training Tips
## Kids and Dogs

1. Easy Walk Harnesses or Gentle Leader head collars give children a lot more control when walking their dogs, especially if they are medium or large breeds.

2. Stop your dog from jumping by turning your back to them and standing tall.

3. When dogs are excited, encourage your children to speak to them in silent actions. Standing still like a tree and turning your back to the dog has worked well for me.

4. Encourage your children to be engaged in the dog's well-being. Giving them the responsibilities of feeding and walking the dog (with supervision) develops confidence and independence while ensuring quality time with the dog at the same time.

5. The Kung Fu Finger can be used to exert downward pressure on the tip of your dog's tailbone. This initiates your dog into the Sequence of Surrender. Use this nonverbal command to calm your dog, or anchor it to a spot. Don't pet it or praise it until it has fully relaxed.

6. Be aware of your energy when you play with your dog. Is it a one-way ticket into canine excitement?

# Meditation

## Telekinetic Connection with Your Pet

Grab a few tennis balls. Sit on the floor near your dog, and place the toys in front of you in a modified Asset Ownership position. Take a few grounding breaths, and tether your attention to the feeling of "being breathed." Allow your sit-bones to sink into the floor. Smell the fuzz of the tennis balls. With a soft but joyful tone, call your dog over and praise them for coming, then become silent again.

Pick up one ball, and look at it. Focus on a memory of playing with your dog. Really visualize it, and hold this focus for over 10 seconds. Your consciousness is generating ripples of excitement. Capitalize on it by calmly inviting your dog into playtime. Ask them to lie down, or use the Kung Fu Finger/Tailbone combo to encourage your dog through the Sequence of Surrender. Once they are lying down, reward them with play. Gently rolling a tennis ball toward them accomplishes this.

Allow yourself to merge with your dog's emotion when they receive the ball. Notice how strongly they feel joy. They don't need to be playing at full throttle to feel this. Allow your dog to do whatever they want with the ball. They might drop it, run off with it, or roll it back to you. Just remain silent, and keep your focus tethered to your breath. When your dog loses focus on the ball, grab another one and look at it. Focus on a strong memory, and repeat the sequence above. Eventually, you might be able to train your dog to lie down across from you and play by rolling the ball back and forth.

# Epilogue

When I find myself in social settings where I'm meeting new people, the topic of career often comes up because it's such a natural ice breaker. I usually respond by saying that I'm an entrepreneur at heart, but I also love teaching mindfulness, meditation, and I work as a master dog trainer.

People tend to pause and soak this in, because it's sort of an unusual combination of interests, yet I've managed to fuse these passions into a thrilling career. After a moment's silence, I almost always receive the same question: what's my favorite breed of dog?

It seems like a simple question, yet in the depths of my being I used to find it impossible to answer. To be perfectly honest, the nature of it actually made me cringe every time, and then rage would surface. Yes, a Peaceful Alpha can experience anger, but it's how we transmute it and what we do next that really counts.

I sat with this feeling for a long time in my meditations. I wanted to uncover the root of my strong feelings for this seemingly innocent trigger. When I discovered the answer—that it's coming from a place of curiosity (a natural state for all beings)—I softened.

I never ask this next question, but I think it is important in the context of where I'm taking you: Would you ever ask a business what their favorite race of human to hire is? Possibly a hundred or so years ago, you might have done so, but the world continues to evolve and recognize the absurdity of this question, so I won't touch it any further, except to say, even within races, regions, religions, and belief systems, all humans have souls, and all souls flow from the same source of energy, our beloved Universe herself. This is how I honestly see it now.

I've had the opportunity to work with thousands of canines, yet I feel that I have only scratched the surface of all the breeds that span the globe. Regardless of this, I do have an answer that I love sharing, though perhaps it might not be the expected one. My favorite kind of dog transcends breed. I love the "second chancers." They could take the form of a street mutt, a rescue dog, or a prized standard poodle in need of a new home. It's what's on their inside and what happens next that makes them my favorite.

These dogs come with unspoken trauma from their first life, and they are often overly sensitive and fearful. In general, they tend to lack trust in humans, and as such, represent an incredibly rewarding opportunity. If you approach them too quickly (or sometimes even at all), they cower and run away. If you reach out to pet them, they hide under the couch or attempt to bite you without warning. These are my favorite kinds of dogs because they have been my best teachers. Working with them requires heightened levels of sensitivity, but melting their fear, earning their trust, and then receiving their love makes you want to do it over and over again.

These "second chancers" taught me how to master my body in space, deepen my levels of attunement, and remain incredibly patient without any expectations. The Secret Language of Dogs is incredibly powerful. It's the only thing I use to connect with these kinds of canines, and in working with them, my level of mastery over this communication style continues to deepen, and my empathy with it.

Like a flower opening to the sun, the moment a dog like this gives me their trust and bonds with me is priceless. That dog's choice to move through their wall of protection and experience their natural state of joy uplifts me beyond measure. Though I have no sophisticated measuring equipment other than my heart, I am certain that the level of love these dogs give is much higher because it is in such profound contrast to what they experienced in their former lives.

Developing a framework and a vocabulary for the Secret Language of Dogs is only possible because of the heightened level of awareness our planet (and her humans) are currently undergoing. In my opinion, humanity is entering an age of elevated consciousness. My vision for humanity is to become the steward of the earth and all her creatures.

In my own life, I have been able to use the Secret Language of Dogs to connect with nature in some unbelievable ways. One morning I was exercising at a park and found myself interpreting the Calming Signals that squirrels were making. I made a few gestures back at them, and two young ones approached me. I decided to sit on a bench, catch some sun, and meditate. Imagine my surprise and delight when a squirrel jumped onto my foot and snuggled in with me for nearly 10 minutes.

As the collective consciousness of our species continues to rise, I predict that wild animals will start to open up to humankind and interact with us in new and friendly ways. They will sense our benevolence, feel our love, and slowly start developing relationships with us. I planted the seed of this idea with my father only a few months ago, and would you believe it, the deer that live in the forests started approaching him a month later? Now, a mother and her babies come by every day. The mom assumes the Angle of Protection, and they all wait while my dad cuts up apples and feeds them from his hand.

My greatest desire is that this book helps people unlock the mystery behind some of their dog's emotionally driven behaviors. You see, just removing that little piece of negative energy from daily life creates a massive uptick in your long term well-being. This is the reward that motivates me.

Thank you for reading this book. May you soon become the Peaceful Alpha your dog loves, needs, and respects.

# Appendix

# List of Figures

# Summary of Training Tips

# Summary of Meditations

# Recommended Reading

Chopra, Deepak. *7 Spiritual Laws of Success: A Practical Guide.* San Rafael, CA: Amber-Allen Publishing/New World Library, 1994.

Dispenza, Joe. *Becoming Supernatural.* Carlsbad, CA: Hay House Inc., 2017.

Easwaran, Eknath. *The Bhagavad Gita.* Tomales, CA: Nilgiri Press, 2007.

Hicks, Esther and Jerry. *The Law of Attraction.* Carlsbad, CA: Hay House Inc., 2006.

Horowitz, Alexandra. *Inside of a Dog: What Dogs See, Smell, and Know.* New York: Scribner, 2010.

Kilcommons, Brian and Sarah Wilson. *Good Owners, Great Dogs.* New York: Grand Central Publishing, 1999.

Millan, Cesar. *Be the Pack Leader: Use Cesar's Way to Transform Your Dog . . . and Your Life.* New York: Crown, 2008.

Owens, Paul. *The Dog Whisperer: A Compassionate, Nonviolent Approach to Dog Training.* Second edition. Holbrook, MA: Adams Media, 2007.

Rugass, Turid. *On Talking Terms with Dogs: Calming Signals.* Second edition. Wenatchee, WA: Dogwise Publishing, 2005.

# Index

**M**
mastery of territory, 148–49
meditation, 50–51
mindfulness, 36, 50–51, 99

**N**
nape of neck, 43, 44, 58
neuroses, 29, 33, 84–85

**O**
overexcitement, 40, 139, 161

**P**
peaceful alpha power, 25, 30, 39, 119, 141, 148, 156
people food, 138–39
potty training, 145–50
power angles, 29–30
power objects, 63–73, 86–93
power of touch, 42–46
praise, 42–43, 128, 147, 164
predictable sequence, 40, 97
presence,15, 34, 53–54, 70, 71
puppy, 26–27, 82, 89,145–56

**R**
raised paw, 65, 97
rescue dog,133
resource guarding, 64–73, 89

**S**
secret language of dogs, 23–24, 31–35, 53, 115, 168

sequence of surrender, 11, 66–67, 133, 144, 164, 165
silence, 37–39, 50, 115, 133, 140
sleep training, 152–53
stop command, 96–101
straight line encounters, 32, 56–57, 61

**T**
teething, 151–52, 155
top-dog status, 63, 64–66
tranquility, 25, 31, 35, 41, 59, 65
transformation, 18, 47, 70, 80, 90–91, 101, 110–12, 131–32, 142, 154–55, 163
trust, 32, 65, 89, 125, 167

**U**
universe, 13, 93, 119, 126, 140

**V**
vibrations, 35, 75, 119, 122, 124

**W**
well-being, 116–19, 122, 148, 168
whining, 12, 63

**Y**
yawning, 15, 24, 27, 29, 54, 109

# About the Author

Photo by Neal Matyas

**Jesse Sternberg** is a mindfulness teacher, meditation instructor, and master dog trainer who has been working with animals for more than 30 years. Jesse offers private training, workshops, and courses on Enlightened Dog Training and The Secret Language of Dogs across North America and online.

For more info visit: **www.peacefulalpha.com**.

FINDHORN PRESS

# Life-Changing Books

Learn more about us and our books at
www.findhornpress.com

For information on the Findhorn Foundation:
www.findhorn.org